D0949576

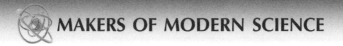
MAKERS OF MODERN SCIENCE

Richard
Feynman

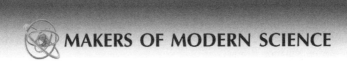

MAKERS OF MODERN SCIENCE

Richard Feynman

Quarks, Bombs, and Bongos

HARRY HENDERSON

CHELSEA HOUSE
PUBLISHERS
An imprint of Infobase Publishing

RICHARD FEYNMAN: Quarks, Bombs, and Bongos

Chelsea House
An imprint of Infobase Publishing
132 West 31st Street
New York NY 10001

Library of Congress Cataloging-in-Publication Data

Henderson, Harry, 1951–
    Richard Feynman: quarks, bombs, and bongos/Harry Henderson.
      p. cm. — (Makers of modern science)
    Includes bibliographical references and index.
    ISBN 978-0-8160-6176-1 (alk. paper)
      1. Feynman, Richard Phillips—Juvenile literature. 2. Physicists—United States—
Biography—Juvenile literature. 3. Nuclear physics—Juvenile literature. I. Title.
II. Series.
    QC16.F49H46 2010
    530.092—dc22
    [B]   2009051487

Text design by Kerry Casey
Composition by Keith Trego
Illustrations by Sholto Ainslie
Photo research by Suzanne M. Tibor
Cover printed by Art Print, Taylor, PA
Book printed and bound by Maple Press, York, PA
Date printed: October 2010
Printed in the United States of America

10 9 8 7 6 5 4 3 2 1

This book is printed on acid-free paper.

CONTENTS

PREFACE

Science is, above all, a great human adventure. It is the process of exploring what Albert Einstein called the "magnificent structure" of nature using observation, experience, and logic. Science comprises the best methods known to humankind for finding reliable answers about the unknown. With these tools, scientists probe the great mysteries of the universe—from black holes and star nurseries to deep-sea hydrothermal vents (and extremophile organisms that survive high temperatures to live in them); from faraway galaxies to subatomic particles such as quarks and antiquarks; from signs of life on other worlds to microorganisms such as bacteria and viruses here on Earth; from how a vaccine works to protect a child from disease to the DNA, genes, and enzymes that control traits and processes from the color of a boy's hair to how he metabolizes sugar.

Some people think that science is rigid and static, a dusty, musty set of facts and statistics to memorize for a test and then forget. Some think of science as antihuman—devoid of poetry, art, and a sense of mystery. However, science is based on a sense of wonder and is all about exploring the mysteries of life and our planet and the vastness of the universe. Science offers methods for testing and reasoning that help keep us honest with ourselves. As physicist Richard Feynman once said, science is above all a way to keep from fooling yourself—or letting nature (or others) fool you. Nothing could be more growth-oriented or more human. Science evolves continually. New bits of knowledge and fresh discoveries endlessly shed light and open perspectives. As a result, science is constantly undergoing revolutions—ever refocusing what scientists have explored before into fresh, new understanding. Scientists like to say science is self-correcting. That is, science is fallible, and scientists can be wrong. It is easy to fool yourself, and it is easy to be fooled by others, but because new facts are constantly flowing in, scientists are continually refining their work to account for as many facts as possible. So science can make mistakes, but it also can correct itself.

Sometimes, as medical scientist Jonas Salk liked to point out, good science thrives when scientists ask the right question about what they observe. "What people think of as the moment of discovery is really the discovery of the question," he once remarked.

There is no one, step-by-step "scientific method" that all scientists use. However, science requires the use of methods that are systematic, logical, and *empirical* (based on objective observation and experience). The goal of science is to explore and understand how nature works—what causes the patterns, the shapes, the colors, the textures, the consistency, the mass, and all the other characteristics of the natural universe that we see.

What is it like to be a scientist? Many people think of stereotypes of the scientist trapped in cold logic or the cartoonlike "mad" scientists. In general, these portrayals are more imagination than truth. Scientists use their brains. They are exceptionally good at logic and critical thinking. This is where the generalizations stop. Although science follows strict rules, it is often guided by the many styles and personalities of the scientists themselves, who have distinct individuality, personality, and style. What better way to explore what science is all about than through the experiences of great scientists?

Each volume of the Makers of Modern Science series presents the life and work of a prominent scientist whose outstanding contributions have garnered the respect and recognition of the world. These men and women were all great scientists, but they differed in many ways. Their approaches to the use of science were different: Niels Bohr was an atomic theorist whose strengths lay in patterns, ideas, and conceptualization, while Wernher von Braun was a hands-on scientist/engineer who led the team that built the giant rocket used by Apollo astronauts to reach the Moon. Some's genius was sparked by solitary contemplation—geneticist Barbara McClintock worked alone in fields of maize and sometimes spoke to no one all day long. Others worked as members of large, coordinated teams. Oceanographer Robert Ballard organized oceangoing ship crews on submersible expeditions to the ocean floor; biologist Jonas Salk established the

Salk Institute to help scientists in different fields collaborate more freely and study the human body through the interrelationships of their differing knowledge and approaches. Their personal styles also differed: biologist Rita Levi-Montalcini enjoyed wearing chic dresses and makeup; McClintock was sunburned and wore baggy denim jeans and an oversized shirt; nuclear physicist Richard Feynman was a practical joker and an energetic bongo drummer.

The scientists chosen represent a spectrum of disciplines and a diversity of approaches to science as well as lifestyles. Each biography explores the scientist's younger years along with education and growth as a scientist; the experiences, research, and contributions of the maturing scientist; and the course of the path to recognition. Each volume also explores the nature of science and its unique usefulness for studying the universe and contains sidebars covering related facts or profiles of interest, introductory coverage of the scientist's field, line illustrations and photographs, a time line, a glossary of related scientific terms, and a list of further resources including books, Web sites, periodicals, and associations.

The volumes in the Makers of Modern Science series offer a factual look at the lives and exciting contributions of the profiled scientists in the hope that readers will see science as a uniquely human quest to understand the universe and that some readers may be inspired to follow in the footsteps of these great scientists.

ACKNOWLEDGMENTS

I would like to thank my editor Frank K. Darmstadt for his patient help and suggestions; Suzie Tibor for her hard work in rounding up the photographs; and as always my wife, Lisa Yount—the best partner and friend I could ever imagine.

INTRODUCTION

A s the stereotype would have it, scientists are "nerds"—brilliant, but obsessed with their work, unfashionably dressed, and often socially awkward.

Richard Feynman, the subject of this volume in the multivolume Makers of Modern Science set for middle school and high school readers, fit that stereotype and also overcame it. A shy high school student, the adult Feynman went on to become a good dancer and a witty conversationalist. His third wife cured his lack of fashion sense. But the "brilliant" part was always true, and Feynman's genius and originality extended beyond physics to biology and computer science and even to the creation of striking artworks and moving poetry.

This brash New York–born American physicist startled the more conservative giants of European physics with his endless ability to improvise. (Indeed in later life he became an accomplished drummer.)

This hands-on approach extended into the heart of Feynman's science. Feynman loved the physical part of physics: the way a spring bent or a pendulum danced. (Chapter 1 will show how Richard's father encouraged this way of learning about science.) Even though he specialized in the most abstract kind of physics—the invisible world of subatomic particles—Feynman had an unusual knack for making that world understandable. He would use his ability to create mental pictures of how particles interacted, devising the diagrams that would give generations of physics students an instant sense of what was going on inside complicated equations.

Feynman and American Science

The story of Richard Feynman is not just the story of an eccentric genius who was also a superb teacher and mentor to a new generation of physicists. It is also very much about American science coming of age in the middle of the 20th century.

By 1900 the United States had become an economic and industrial powerhouse second to none. The nation had more railroads than all of Europe combined and was the world's leading producer of steel. American inventors were adept at turning scientific discoveries into new devices that created whole industries—Thomas Edison's lightbulbs and power systems and Bell's telephone had ushered in the age of electricity.

In science itself, however, Europe remained the center of activity. It was Europeans who had been making the key discoveries of the 19th century, ranging from Louis Pasteur's uniting of biology and chemistry to Charles Darwin's theory of evolution. The same held true in physics. In the physics of the universe at large, Albert Einstein's theory of relativity had replaced Newton's gravitational theory with a new concept of curved space-time. Meanwhile the physics of the tiniest things (atoms and their component particles) had burst into activity with the discovery of radioactivity in the 1890s by Marie and Pierre Curie and the discovery of subatomic particles (protons and electrons). Chapter 2 describes how young Richard Feynman had to decide how to pursue a career in physics as exciting new discoveries from Europe were reverberating through the field.

In particular, the 1920s brought the new science of quantum physics, led by Danish physicist Niels Bohr and German physicists Erwin Schrödinger and Werner Heisenberg. Chapter 3 introduces these new theories that Feynman would be among the first Americans to master. Chapter 4 recounts how Feynman and Wheeler developed their first theory of electron interaction while Feynman developed the mathematical techniques he would use throughout his career.

War and Love

By the end of the 1930s, a world war was on the horizon even as news came of a fateful experiment: the splitting of the atom (fission) and the possibility of creating a weapon of unprecedented destructive power. As described in chapter 5, Feynman would play an important role in the birth of the atomic bomb and the nuclear age. At the same time, he would watch Arline Greenbaum, the woman he loved, die slowly of tuberculosis, while he tried to steal every hour he could to share with her.

With the war ended and Arline gone, Feynman seemed at a loss about how to continue his career. As told in chapter 6, Feynman would gradually regain his interest in physics while being courted by famous universities. This chapter features the work for which Feynman would receive his Nobel Prize. He developed a method for calculating particle interactions that eliminated the troubling mathematical sinkholes that plagued earlier approaches. Along with this method came the now-famous Feynman diagrams that summarized interactions in a way a bit like the circles and arrows used by football coaches to explain plays.

A Many-Faceted Person

The last three chapters look at other important aspects of Feynman as a person and as a scientist. Chapter 7 describes a variety of important research areas explored by Feynman in later years. For example, he made considerable progress in explaining the weird behavior of liquid helium. Feynman also made surprising contributions to the design of new kinds of computers, as well as proposing nanotechnology, which is one of today's hottest research areas.

Chapter 8 looks at a very important if sometimes neglected aspect of Feynman—his ability as a teacher. No undergraduate who attended Feynman's regular physics lectures would ever forget the way he combined clear explanations with a sense of how science actually worked and why science was important. Feynman also worked to improve math and science textbooks and to further science education for the general public.

This chapter also explores another side of Feynman, one that is both fascinating and a bit controversial. As the years passed, Feynman gained an ever-growing reputation as a trickster and a social "operator." Indeed there are enough anecdotes about Feynman's personal life to fill several books—and they have!

By the 1980s, Feynman was battling the cancer that would eventually kill him but not before he used one last brilliant, theatrical demonstration to explain to Congress and the American people why the space shuttle *Challenger* had exploded. Chapter 9 tells the story of how Feynman battled NASA bureaucrats to warn that the space program had gone off course.

Finally, the book's conclusion sums up the lasting legacy of a remarkable scientist—and a unique personality.

1

The Joy of
Finding Out

Richard Phillips Feynman (1918–88) was born in Far Rockaway, in the New York City borough of Queens. Although close to Manhattan, Far Rockaway in the 1920s was more like a village, clustered along a section of beach on a peninsula on the south shore of Long Island. It was a great place to grow up. There were yards, empty lots, numerous paths for children to wander, and, most of all, the beach. Every summer, thousands of New York residents would come to escape the stifling heat of the city. For local residents like young Richard Feynman, though, the beach was a year-round playground.

Later, Feynman would reflect on his childhood surroundings in the following excerpt from his Feynman Lectures:

Richard Feynman as a boy with his parents (California Institute of Technology, Archives)

> *If we stand on the shore and look at the sea, we see the water, the waves breaking, the foam, the sloshing motion of the water, the sound, the air, the winds and the clouds, the sun and the blue sky, and light; there is sand and there are rocks of various hardness and permanence, color and texture. There are animals and seaweed, hunger and disease, and the observer on the beach; there may even be happiness and thought.*

Physics is the study of change, movement, interaction, the flow of energy, the transformation of matter from one state to another. From a young age, Feynman learned to pay attention to the changing pageant of nature, to make observations, and to ask interesting questions.

The Essence of Mathematics

In learning how to observe and work with patterns, Feynman considered his father to be his first and perhaps greatest teacher. Melville Feynman made a living as a businessperson, but he had a passion for science. In his 1966 talk, "What Is Science?" Richard Feynman recalls the following:

> *When my mother was carrying me, it is reported—I am not directly aware of the conversation—my father said that "if it's a boy, he'll be a scientist." How did he do it? He never told me I should be a scientist. He was not a scientist; he was a businessman, a sales manager of a uniform company, but he read about science and loved it.*

Like many Jewish immigrants to the United States, Melville Feynman believed in the value of hard work and had great respect (and even love) for learning. As the 20th century progressed, science in particular began to stand out as a desirable career for the children of ambitious immigrants. Science seemed to be the source of progress itself, whether expressed in new industries such as radio or in medical advances. Indeed a few square miles of Jewish neighborhoods in New York would produce an outpouring of scientists and doctors, despite the discrimination that Jews still faced in college admissions and jobs.

Melville delighted in introducing his son to mathematics and science. When "Ritty" was still very small, his father obtained a collection of colored bathroom tiles from a company's surplus stock. He arranged them in long rows like dominoes and let his son knock one over at the end of the arrangement and watch the mayhem spread down the orderly rows. The young boy delighted in this operation, which perhaps foreshadowed the nuclear chain reactions he would be concerned with at Los Alamos.

But Melville also used the game to teach about patterns and the discipline needed to work with them. He introduced the rule that the tiles must be put in order, one white, two blues, then another white, and so on. In "What Is Science?" Feynman later recalled that:

. . . my mother, who is a much more feeling woman, began to realize the insidiousness of his efforts and said, "Mel, please let the poor child put a blue tile if he wants to." My father said, "No, I want him to pay attention to patterns. It is the only thing I can do that is mathematics at this earliest level."

This showed considerable insight on Melville's part. To many people, mathematics means working with numbers—computation. But for professionals, mathematics is mainly about working with patterns and only later applying those patterns to actual numbers in order to solve practical problems.

In this story, Feynman also recognized his mother's part in his upbringing. Commenting on his mother's influence in *What Do You Care What Other People Think?* Feynman notes that, "In particular, she had a wonderful sense of humor, and I learned from her that the highest forms of understanding we can achieve are laughter and human compassion." In Feynman's later life, this would be reflected in how he often made himself the object of his own jokes and did not let the importance of his work make him too self-important.

An Early Lesson in Physics

Melville also introduced his son to physics. One day Richard noticed that when he had a ball in his toy wagon and pulled the wagon forward, the ball would roll to the back. He asked his father about this and he replied:

That, nobody knows. The general principle is that things that are moving try to keep on moving, and things that are standing still tend to stand still, unless you push them hard. This tendency is called inertia, but no one knows why it's true.

Feynman later remarked that this showed a deep understanding on his father's part. Many teachers would have been satisfied by simply explaining *inertia*: the ball resists being pulled forward by the wagon, so the back of the wagon "catches up" to it. Perhaps the teacher would also talk about the role of friction. But Melville did more: he pointed out that no one knew why matter behaved this way. And indeed, the nature of mass and inertia remains among the deepest mysteries of physics. This lesson taught young Richard that science is not just about facts and explanations but is also an inquiry into the essential nature of things.

Learning How to See

Richard's father taught him the essence of science in another way. One of Richard's young friends asked him the name of a particular bird. When Richard said he did not know, the other boy said, "It's a brown-throated thrush. Your father doesn't teach you anything!"

But Richard knew this was not true. His father had already told him about the difference between naming a thing and truly understanding it.

> *You can know the name of that bird in all the languages of the world, but when you're finished, you'll know absolutely nothing about the bird. You'll only know about humans in different places, and what they call the bird. So let's look at the bird and see what it's doing—that's what counts.*

In thinking about physical phenomena, Richard Feynman would never forget to look at "what the bird is doing."

Feynman's interest in science was encouraged in many other ways. He and his father frequently visited the Museum of Natural History in Manhattan, where there were an endless supply of interesting animal displays, fossils, and minerals to be examined.

When Feynman was 11 the family moved to the nearby town of Cedarhurst. At Cedarhurst Elementary School he got into an argument with the science teacher about how light rays come out of a bulb. The teacher drew the rays as parallel lines, but Feynman knew intuitively that was wrong—the rays would come out radially in all directions. When the boy objected, the teacher refused to continue the discussion. Here was another important lesson for a future scientist: trust intuition (checked by observation) and do not accept something just because some authority insists on it. Feynman would emphasize this in his own lecturing and outreach to the public.

A Boy and His Laboratory

Like many other boys of the time, Feynman received a chemistry set one year for his birthday. Unfortunately some older boys got a

☆ A Generation of Tinkerers

Many scientists and engineers who grew up in the 1920s and 1930s would look fondly back on their youth as a time when there were endless opportunities to build, tinker, and discover. One reason was that new technologies such as radio excited the young imagination. Countless youngsters built little radios by wiring resistors and capacitors to crystals that could receive the invisible waves that brought speech and music from hundreds of miles away if the conditions were right.

The other reason for the golden age of tinkering was that early radios, like the automobiles of the time, were understandable by people without specialized training. Today's electronic devices pack their circuits into tiny chips. If it breaks, something like a computer is not really "fixed"—rather, once the defective part (such as a hard drive) is found, the whole part must be replaced.

For Feynman's generation, however, the mechanically inclined could tear down a car engine and rebuild it from scratch. The scientific tinkerer could build a working crystal radio set from a handful of parts or play with electric motors, switches, and relays. Every part shown in a circuit diagram was a recognizable, physical object—a tube, a switch, a capacitor, a resistor, and so on.

The result of this experience was a generation who went into fields such as electrical engineering with plenty of hands-on experience and confidence in their ability to design new devices or fix problems with existing ones. This extended even to the millions of U.S. soldiers who drove their trucks and jeeps into battle in World War II. Observers noted that while most German soldiers had to wait for specialized repair crews when their vehicles broke down, the average G.I. could fix most automotive problems because he had spent much of his teenage years tinkering with cars.

Even today, the "tinkerer gene" is far from dead. Many young people are fascinated by robots and can use a variety of kits to build them. They are also comfortable with computers and software and can "tinker" in the virtual world, building elaborate settings for online games or worlds, such as *Second Life.*

hold of it and dumped all the chemicals together onto the sidewalk to see what would happen. This setback was only temporary: Feynman resolved to build and equip his own laboratory in the privacy of his bedroom.

At the time, the United States was entering the Great Depression, a time of severe economic hardship where money for "extra" items was hard to come by. However this was also a time when an increasing number of families relied on radio for inexpensive entertainment. The early tube radios often broke, and young Feynman saw an opportunity. He would learn how to fix them. Besides, each radio presented a puzzle, a challenge, and Feynman loved to figure things out. He learned to check connections, wire antennas, change tubes, and replace parts such as a burnt-out resistor.

One time a man brought him a radio and complained that it made a terrible noise while it was warming up. Feynman reasoned that because the noise eventually went away, it must have something to do with the order in which the tubes warmed up. He switched two tubes and the noise vanished. (Later Feynman used the incident for an amusing little story "The Boy Who Fixes Radios by Thinking.")

Feynman poured his radio earnings into buying more equipment for his laboratory, which was greatly expanded when the family returned to Far Rockaway. He soon had a good selection of chemicals, lenses for optical experiments, and even equipment for developing photographs. The lab was also wired into the house's electric circuits, as well as being equipped with batteries.

Once Feynman heard from his father that electrochemistry was an important new field in industry. Feynman did not quite know what electrochemistry involved, so he experimented by putting live wires into piles of various chemicals—without much success except for producing the occasional foul-smelling gas. (In industry, electrochemistry is used for such applications as plating one layer of metal on another and for designing batteries and fuel cells.)

Other electrical experiments were more productive. Late one night, Feynman's parents came home and were startled by a loud clanging as they opened the door. Thanks to their son, the Feynmans now had their very own burglar alarm.

High School Physics and Mathematics

In 1931 Feynman entered Far Rockaway High School. Naturally he was most interested in his science courses, studying general science, physics, and chemistry. He also served as vice president of the physics club.

Abram Bader, one physics teacher, was particularly influential in Feynman's thinking. He explained a key principle called *least action*. A common example involves a moving object such as a fly ball in baseball. The ball has two kinds of energy. First, there is the kinetic (moving) energy given it by the bat. There is also potential energy, which is due to gravity. As the ball rises, some of its kinetic energy is turned into potential energy. (That is, the ball has less forward motion but has gained altitude.) When the ball reaches the highest point of its flight, that potential energy begins to turn back into kinetic energy as the ball heads down toward the ground (or the fielder's waiting glove).

By subtracting the potential energy from the kinetic energy and taking the average, one arrives at the actual path the object will take. The principle of least action says that for a given flight time, there is a single unique path the object will take, which is always the shortest path. This principle applies to much more than balls or other flying objects. It can also be used to calculate the movement of a charged particle in an electromagnetic field or even the movement of electrons within atoms.

This principle and others impressed young Feynman with the elegance of physics—the way components of a phenomenon fit together and the way nature so neatly "solves" the equations in the paths that emerge for objects as simple as balls or as seemingly complex as atoms. As Feynman told his biographer Jagdish Mehra: "I reacted to it then and there, that this was a miraculous and marvelous thing to be able to express the laws in such an unusual fashion."

Bader also encouraged Feynman to study calculus, the most essential mathematical tool for physics. Feynman kept a notebook that he filled with interesting equations as he delved more deeply into higher mathematics.

Meanwhile, in his regular classes Feynman took algebra, geometry, and trigonometry but found he had already gotten well beyond what was being taught in those subjects. Indeed, the geometry teacher was soon inviting Feynman to teach some of the material to the class!

The young "math whiz" also enjoyed competing in something called the Interscholastic Algebra League. Each team of five students was given a set of problems to solve. The real challenge was that there was a time limit (often 45 seconds). The problems were designed so that it would take too long to solve them just by following the rules taught in algebra class. To solve the problem in time, the student would have to, as we say today, "think outside the box."

It turned out that Feynman was very good at such thinking. He often solved the problem in a few seconds, writing his answer on the page and circling it, while the other competitors were still trying to figure out how to proceed.

Sometimes, though, Feynman would have a little trouble with mathematics. For example, when he was first introduced to solid geometry, he could solve problems by following the rules the teacher gave. However, he did not really know what he was doing, which bothered him considerably. After a few weeks, though, he suddenly realized that the figures on the paper actually represented "real" three-dimensional objects. Now he could visualize the shapes, and his intuition took over from there.

Something other than science was also sparking young Feynman's interest. Back when he was 13, he had met a girl, Arline Greenbaum, who even at that age impressed the boys with her attractiveness and sharp wit. By the time he was getting ready to leave high school, Feynman was becoming decidedly interested in Arline—but many other boys had a similar interest. Like most of his male classmates, Feynman was awkward around girls, even as he began to learn the rules to ease participation in social activities.

Feynman would soon be entering a much more complex scientific and social world.

Along the Infinite Corridor

A s high school drew to an end and Feynman considered where he would go to college, he first applied to Columbia University. However, despite his fine work in science and mathematics, Feynman's low scores in other subjects led to his being rejected. He then applied to and was accepted by the Massachusetts Institute of Technology (MIT).

A New Kind of School

Founded in Cambridge, Massachusetts, in 1865 by the geologist and "natural philosopher" William Barton Rogers, MIT was a response to the rapid growth in science and industry in the United States in the mid-19th century. Traditional universities emphasized liberal arts, with a sprinkling of mathematics and science.

While this might be adequate preparation for a career in fields such as law or government, educators such as Rogers believed that a new kind of institution was needed to train American scientists and engineers.

The new institution's brochure (quoted by Fred Hapgood in *Up the Infinite Corridor*) gives a good indication of what it originally offered:

> *a complete course of instruction and training, suited to the various practical professions of the Mechanician, the Civil Engineer, the Builder and Architect, the Mining Engineer, and the Practical Chemist; and, at the same time, to meet the more limited aims of such as desire to secure a scientific preparation for special industrial pursuits, such as the direction of Mills, Machine Shops, Railroads, Mines, Chemical Works, Glass, Potter and Paper manufacturers, and of Dyeing,*

The Rogers Building at the Massachusetts Institute of Technology (MIT) as it appeared in the 1890s. Chartered in 1861, MIT symbolized the coming of age of the United States as a leader in science and technology. (Library of Congress)

Print, and Gas works; and for the practice of Navigation and Surveying, of Telegraphy, Photography, and Electrotyping, and the various other Arts having their foundations in the exact sciences.

Instead of emphasizing lectures, professors at this practical school would focus on laboratory work and seminars. Students would learn about science by doing research and about engineering by working with the latest technology. (This type of education was already underway in Germany, which was becoming one of the world's leading industrial and technical powers.)

The Engineering Culture

As described by Fred Hapgood in *Up the Infinite Corridor*, the focus of MIT during the first part of the 20th century was on developing a trained elite of engineers who would build the machines needed by ever-growing industry. Until the 1930s, this especially meant electrical engineering—generators and power systems, but also equipment for the telephone and radio industries. As Hapgood notes, this was serious business:

> For the first half of the century MIT graduates were not expected to be inventors or innovators (though of course many were), but tweakers, incrementalists, who worked to move the productivity of industry's capital goods one or two percentage points a year. They might be asked to redesign an 80-line telephone relay so it could handle 160 calls (and then 320, and then 640, etc.) or to expand the range of wattages available in lightbulbs from four models to six, or to move the horsepower of an internal combustion engine one class higher.

After about 1940, fueled by the wartime development of radar and microwave technology, and eventually computers, electronics would come to the forefront at MIT. By the 1960s the development of minicomputers made hands-on computer experience available to students. Talented if rather obsessive programmers created their own software and got the machines to do new things—play games, even generate music. These programmers became known as hackers, a word that was later misapplied to people who broke into computers and stole information.

By the 1920s, though, many MIT classes had settled into performing routine demonstrations and exercises with machines such as engines and electrical generators. (Electronic devices such as the radios Feynman tinkered with were just starting to make their appearance.) However by the time Feynman arrived in the mid-1930s, the course of study at MIT was undergoing changes. Under the innovative engineer and administrator Vannevar Bush, courses began to emphasize a deeper understanding of physical processes. The application of mathematical principles to design was also being explored. (Bush himself had designed a mechanical computer that could solve complex equations.)

MIT was both exhilarating and a bit overwhelming for the bright high school graduates who arrived there. Even the place itself could be intimidating. Traditional college campuses often have buildings of different styles widely scattered among paths and trees. At MIT, however, buildings were numbered rather than named and were linked by a long enclosed main corridor that became known as the Infinite Corridor. Fred Hapgood notes that:

> Building 7 feeds into 3 and 3 sits next to 10 and 10 next to 4 and so on. A stranger rushing to make a scheduled appointment might think the design calculated to drive him crazy, but a visitor free to wander might also be impressed by the freedom of direction, the unpredictability of association, the richness of interconnection. Any point in the campus seems equally near or far from any other. The same degree of associative freedom might be felt in wandering through the consciousness of an exceptionally vital mind.

Like many first-year college students, Feynman found that he had more freedom to pursue his interests, but he would have to meet higher standards as well. The competition to prove oneself at MIT could be fierce, with both friendships and rivalries rapidly arising in the academic pressure cooker.

Mathematics or Physics?

As he got used to the MIT environment, the most important choice Feynman faced was what to study. At first he seemed to be more interested in mathematics than in physics. Because he had mastered so much of mathematics already, he took an examination that allowed him to skip first-year calculus and begin the second-year course. However he gradually became dissatisfied with his mathematics courses. While one might expect mathematics at MIT to focus on the practical needs of engineering, Feynman found that not to be the case. The mathematics curriculum was too abstract for his taste, appearing to have little connection with the real world.

As James Gleick recounts in *Genius: The Life and Science of Richard Feynman,* Feynman finally went to the head of the mathematics department and asked him: "Sir, what is the use of mathematics if not to teach more mathematics?" He replied dismissively that if Feynman wanted a practical use for mathematics, he could always get a job calculating insurance rates.

What Feynman really wanted, though, was to use mathematical and experimental tools to explore the secrets of the physical world. Physics at the time was hardly a mainstream profession in the United States. There were only a handful of American physicists who could be compared to their European counterparts. Job prospects for physicists were also limited. Nevertheless, Feynman enrolled in a physics course.

Hands-on Physics

Fortunately, Feynman had arrived at a time when American science seemed to be waking up. Under department head John C. Slater, the MIT physics department was being revamped and expanded. In part these changes were being driven by urgent pleas from industries such as telephone and radio, which needed physics to understand how to design the new circuits needed to carry ever-growing communications traffic.

The mixture of theory and practice in the new courses greatly appealed to Feynman. Feynman particularly enjoyed the hands-on approach. In the physics laboratory Feynman was given a simple-looking experiment. A metal ring was hung from a nail on the wall. As he would later tell Mehra, the object of the experiment was to "measure the period [time the ring took to swing back and forth], calculate the period from the shape, and see if they agree." As quoted by Mehra, Feynman took unexpected pleasure from this experiment:

> *I thought this was the best doggone thing. I liked the other experiments, but they involved sparks and other hocus-pocus, which was too easy. With all that equipment you could measure the acceleration due to gravity. The remarkable thing is that physics is so good, in that not only can you figure out something carefully prepared but something so natural as a lousy old ring hanging off a hook—that impressed me!*

A Not So Well-Rounded Student

Outside of science, Feynman viewed required courses in humanities—subjects such as literature, philosophy, and art—with a mixture of suspicion and irritation. He considered many of the ideas in these fields to be illogical or pretentious. It seemed to him that while philosophers might ask interesting questions, they had no reliable method for finding any answers. He did dabble a bit in writing poetry. In general, Feynman seemed to skate through these courses without learning much, while managing to get decent marks. Only later in life would he return to the arts as a way to express his creativity.

Even at MIT, student life was not all lectures and study. Perhaps to offset the reputation of young engineers as being much more comfortable with a slide rule than a dance partner, MIT tried hard to encourage students to develop a social life and to be "well-rounded." Like other schools, MIT had fraternities that were segregated: only two admitted Jews.

In some colleges students wanting to join a fraternity might be subject to hazing, such as being forced to drink large quantities of beer. At MIT, however, the tests were a bit more intellectual. As Feynman wrote,

> *we were sent on a scavenger hunt yesterday . . . a lot of fun until I got back to the damn fraternity. I had to get a wiffle tree [a pivoting bar attached to a harness], a ball-bearing mousetrap (i.e., a cat, male), an egg plant, a projectile that when uniformly accelerated from a 30-foot cannon will*

acquire a velocity of 500,000 foot-pounds, and the number of windows in the Suffolk County jail divided by the square root of two to ten places.

The fraternities also served a serious purpose. Students learned to live together and help one another. A bright but socially awkward student such as Feynman might have dates arranged by more popular students in exchange for some mathematics tutoring. Attendance at dances was compulsory, but Feynman began to look forward to these activities and became more confident around the young women who often visited from other schools. The most important visitor for Feynman was Arline, who was tutoring his younger sister Joan in piano and also increasingly appearing as Feynman's date.

3

Entering the Quantum World

At the time Feynman entered MIT, physics for most people meant the laws of motion that govern how familiar objects behave when they are pushed around by outside forces. Everyday objects such as flying balls could be understood completely using the *classical mechanics* first developed by Isaac Newton in the 17th century. Generally speaking, this is the physics of things that people can see, moving at speeds that are more or less comprehensible.

What most interested physicists in the early 20th century was the physics of things that moved very fast, were very small, or both. When Feynman began his studies in physics in the mid-1930s, physicists were still trying to catch up with two revolutions from earlier in the century. One of these was Einstein's theory of *relativity,* which relates space, time, matter, and energy in a consistent but surprising way (for example, with space that bends or curves and fast-moving objects that gain in mass and shrink in length).

As difficult as relativity was for many students to understand, by the 1930s it had been pretty well assimilated into science's picture of the universe, where it neatly filled in the places where Newton's classical theory was inadequate—for example, explaining the complex path of the planet Mercury deep in the Sun's gravitational field.

For Feynman and his teachers and colleagues, the more challenging arena dealt not with large bodies out in space but with objects that are often close to hand, but incredibly small. This is the world of nuclear physics, which studies the structure of atoms, the particles that make them up, and processes such as *radioactive* decay and collisions between atoms and fast-moving particles.

Changing Pictures of the Atom

Atoms themselves were nothing new. About 2,500 years ago, the Greek philosopher Democritus concluded that at some point there must be something that cannot be cut into anything smaller. He called these hypothetical objects atoms (*"atom"* is a Greek word meaning "not cuttable").

Atomic theory did not seem to be of practical use until modern chemistry began to develop in the 17th century. The British chemist Robert Boyle proposed that matter is made up of combinations of atoms. In the next century, the French scientist Antoine Lavoisier identified certain substances (such as carbon or oxygen) as being fundamental elements that could not be broken down into simpler substances.

Early in the 19th century, the British chemist John Dalton tied atomic theory to chemistry by proposing that each element consists of a particular kind of atom (which is why it could not be broken down further chemically). As the century progressed, chemists worked out how atoms combined to form chemical compounds. They found that atoms had different masses, ranging from tiny hydrogen to (relatively) huge *uranium*. It also became clear that atoms could combine with other atoms in certain ways but not in others. However, no one knew why this might be so.

Inside the Atom

By the 1890s, when Feynman's father came to America as a child, many physicists felt their work was pretty much wrapped up. Indeed, the famous British physicist Lord Kelvin is reported to have said "There is nothing new to be discovered in physics now. All that remains is more and more precise measurement." (This is widely quoted but no definitive source has been found.) At any rate, there seemed to be little more to learn about atoms, since they were believed to be featureless and without internal structure.

However, just before the turn of the 20th century came startling new discoveries about atoms. In 1897, the British physicist J. J. Thomson studied the cathode rays that came from a tube like that used later in televisions. These "rays" (which were actually tiny charged particles called *electrons*) turned out to be part of every atom—and atoms were not supposed to have parts at all!

Thomson visualized the atom as a sort of "plum pudding" where the electrons were like raisins sprinkled randomly throughout. However in 1909 another British physicist Ernest Rutherford bombarded gold foil with *ions* (charged atoms) and discovered more about the atom's internal structure. The way a very few of the ions were deflected from the gold atoms showed that atoms must have a tiny central core or nucleus. The fact that so few ions were deflected meant that the atom was mostly empty space.

When Feynman was first studying physics in high school, his textbooks no doubt showed a picture of the atom that is still used today. In the center is the nucleus (which was later discovered to consist of two particles, *protons* and *neutrons*). Around the nucleus were the electrons, a particular number for each *element*. The diagram looked very much like that of the solar system, with the Sun surrounded by planets.

Wave or Particle?

The next logical question for physicists to ask was this: why were electrons arranged in such an orderly way? Why did each "shell" have a specific number of slots into which electrons might be fitted?

Max Planck discovered that light energy came in discrete "chunks" called quanta.
(Library of Congress)

Or, more fundamentally, why did not all the electrons, their negative charges being tugged by the positive charge of the central protons, crash into the nucleus and destroy the atom?

The beginning of a solution to this riddle was contributed in 1900 by Max Planck, the noted German physicist. He was trying to explain what happens when a *black body* (a theoretical object that absorbs all wavelengths of light) is gradually heated. It turns out that as the temperature increases, the color of the light emitted moves smoothly along the spectrum from invisible infrared to blazing white and beyond to ultraviolet, the shortest waves. At each temperature the majority of the waves have a specific wavelength, with smaller numbers of waves being shorter or longer, forming a smooth curve when plotted on a chart. However, according to the accepted theory of light as consisting of waves, energy should be easier to emit at short wavelengths, regardless of the temperature. Why are not all hot objects blazing in invisible violet?

Planck solved the problem by assuming that the black body could only radiate energy in a fixed amount called a *quantum.* In

1905, Albert Einstein generalized this idea to show that the behavior of light interacting with electrons could also be explained by considering it to be made up of discrete particles, each containing a quantum of energy. (It is this work that would win him the Nobel Prize in 1922, rather than his more famous theories of relativity.)

While this new particle theory worked well, it created yet another puzzle for physicists. The great 19th-century Scottish physicist James Clerk Maxwell had developed a very successful theory of electromagnetic *waves*, including light. This theory explained, for example, how light is diffracted or bent by a prism. Maxwell's wave equations explained all these "large scale" interactions. However the interactions of light and electrons within atoms often seemed to involve solid particles. What was the relationship between these particles and the larger scale waves?

The Danish physicist Niels Bohr had the next insight: Bohr applied Einstein's quantum theory to electrons instead of light. If electrons could only absorb or emit energy in fixed amounts (quanta),

Niels Bohr (left) and Albert Einstein seated at Paul Ehrenfest's home in Brussels, 1930. By then Bohr's quantum atom and Einstein's theory of relativity had revolutionized physics from the very small to the immensely large. (Paul Ehrenfest, AIP Emilio Segrè Visual Archives)

the electrons could not spiral down into the nucleus, shedding energy as they went. Instead there was a slot or "orbital" corresponding to each energy level. An electron could jump between slots only if it gained or lost a quantum of energy. But because only one electron could fit in each slot, electrons tended to stay put—and thus most atoms were stable. Further, this behavior explained why each kind of atom had its own characteristic pattern of lines in its spectrum.

A Perplexing Experiment

A simple but intriguing experiment shows how light can be both a wave and a particle. Two screens are placed some distance apart. The first screen has a single pinhole, while the second screen has two pinholes spaced on either side. Finally, a third screen is placed to catch the light coming through the holes in the second screen.

If a light is shined through the hole in the first screen toward the second screen, alternating light and dark bands will appear on the third screen. This is just what is expected if light behaves like waves. (Consider a wave in a pond hitting two rocks and breaking up into separate, overlapping waves.) The bands come from the two waves alternately reinforcing each other and interfering (canceling each other out).

Where things get strange is when particles (electrons or photons) are fired one at a time through the hole in the first screen. If one hole in the second screen is plugged up, the photons "pile up" on the third screen right behind the open hole. This is how particles would be expected to behave.

However, what happens if both of the holes in the second screen are left open and the particles are still fired one at a time? One would expect the particles to pile up in equal amounts behind the two holes (assuming they are spaced correctly). Instead, a pattern of alternating bands is seen, just as with the wave experiment. The particles seem to interact with each other, reinforcing or interfering just like waves!

This experiment shows that light particles (photons) or electrons can act as either particles or waves, depending on how one arranges to observe them. The wave can also be interpreted as the probability that the particle will be found at a particular point.

Competing Theories

Bohr's quantum-based theory created a sensible picture of the atom. However, there remained the question of why particular energy levels resulted in particular orbits for the electrons. The French physicist Louis de Broglie went back to wave theory for the answer. There are certain places where waves "break down" into proportional

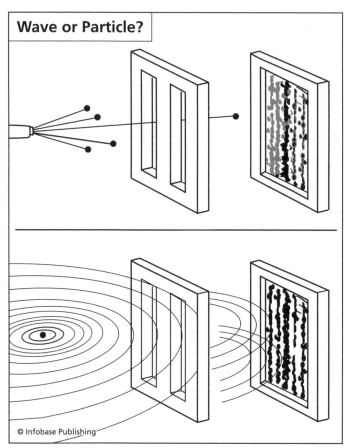

Wave or Particle?

Much of the development of modern physics has focused on two different ways to see energy such as light—particles (photons) or waves. As shown here, oncoming light particles show wave-type interference patterns.

© Infobase Publishing

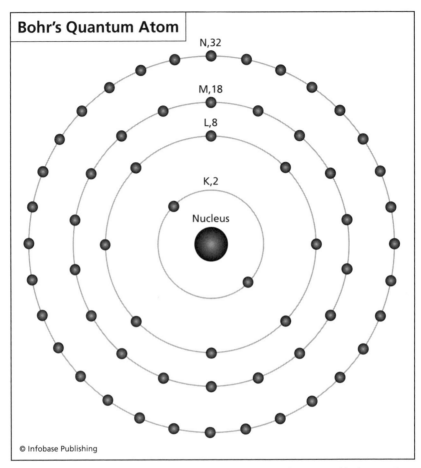

Bohr's Quantum Atom

N,32
M,18
L,8
K,2
Nucleus

In a picture of the atom still familiar to chemistry students, electrons orbit the atomic nucleus only in fixed "shells," determined by discrete energy levels, or quanta. (The first four shells are lettered K, L, M, and N.)

smaller waves, called harmonics. (For example, if a guitar string is touched lightly over the 12th fret while it is plucked, it will produce a harmonic note.)

De Broglie suggested that the electron orbits were like waves wrapped around the atom. If a quantum of energy is absorbed, the wave responds by changing length according to the harmonic principle. Later experiments by American and British physicists showed that electrons being scattered from crystals showed such wavelike behavior. The Austrian physicist Erwin Schrödinger formalized this theory in a comprehensive equation, which earned him the 1933 Nobel Prize in physics.

There was still a problem, however. De Broglie and Schrödinger had believed that the waves they calculated represented the actual distribution of electrical charge in the electron. However as waves in a pond spread out, they lose their energy and eventually vanish—but electrons in an atom must keep moving or the atom would disintegrate.

The German physicist Max Born came up with a different way of thinking about the waves. He decided that they did not represent the

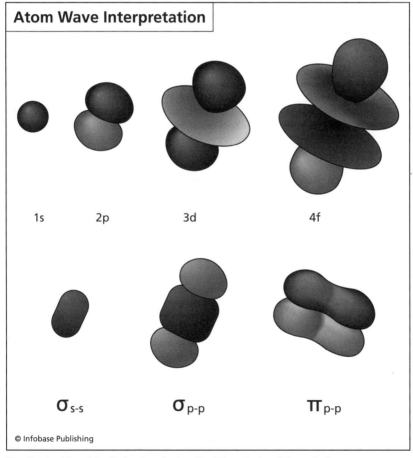

Atom Wave Interpretation

1s   2p   3d   4f

$\sigma_{s\text{-}s}$ $\sigma_{p\text{-}p}$ $\pi_{p\text{-}p}$

© Infobase Publishing

The fixed orbits of the Bohr atom look quite different when interpreted as waves according to quantum mechanics. No longer fixed points, the electrons are shown as probabilities in atomic (top) and molecular (bottom) orbitals.

distribution of electromagnetic energy. Rather, they represented the chance or probability that the electron could be found in a particular location. In effect, this allowed the electron to be both something "solid" (a tiny particle) and yet behave in a wavelike way when considered in large numbers.

Meanwhile, in 1925, the German physicist Werner Heisenberg proposed a different mathematical approach. Instead of trying to visualize the actual motion of the electron or treating it like a wave, Heisenberg and his colleagues compiled sets of numbers that represented different "states" of the electron with regard to its energy, momentum, or spin. When these numbers were arranged in squares called matrices and certain mathematical operations performed, physicists could predict other quantities that could later be confirmed by experiment.

How far had physics come by the mid-1930s, when Feynman was beginning his college studies? Physicists had been used to thinking of light as waves, only to find that sometimes they needed to consider light as particles (photons) containing quanta of energy. On the other hand, the electron, which had been discovered as a particle, needed wave theory to explain some of its behavior. And in 1928, the British physicist Paul Dirac completed the equation that applied Einstein's relativistic mechanics to electrons (which, while tiny, can move almost as fast as light). Dirac's book *The Principles of Quantum Mechanics* (particularly its 1935 edition) became one of Feynman's closest companions at MIT.

Feynman's Quantum Leap

While he was still majoring in mathematics, Feynman roomed with two senior students who were taking an advanced course in physics that had been designed by John Slater, the head of the physics department. Feynman often listened to the older students discussing problems from the course. After a few months of this, Feynman felt bold enough to participate in the discussion. Often Feynman had read of an equation or a mathematical trick that could solve the problem. Meanwhile Feynman picked up much of the higher-level physics.

Having decided to major in physics, Feynman decided he knew enough to tackle the advanced course himself. He would leap over the intervening courses rather in the way an energized electron could jump across the space between energy levels in an atom.

While registering for the advanced class, Feynman met another bright sophomore named Ted Welton who had steeped himself in relativity just as Feynman had already absorbed a lot of quantum theory. The two young men came to admire each other's intellect and decided they would make a good study team.

During the first semester, the course was taught not by Slater but by a young physicist, Julius Stratton. While Stratton was a capable physicist (and a future president of MIT), he sometimes lost track of where he was in the lecture. When this happened, he would turn to the class and ask, "Mr. Feynman, how did you handle this problem?" Feynman would then take over the lecture from that point.

As quoted in a MIT press release in connection with Feynman's book *The Meaning of It All*, Feynman's fellow student (and later distinguished nuclear physicist) Herman Feshbach noted that the flamboyant Feynman of later times was not yet in evidence in those early years at MIT. Feynman was "very conscientious, very square, very dedicated to physics."

"The Last Word in Cosmic Rays"

The advanced course had a limited amount of quantum mechanics, but it was not enough to satisfy Feynman and Welton. Philip Morse, who taught the second semester, soon invited them to join another student for special tutoring in quantum theory. Morse gave Feynman some tough, "real world" applications in quantum mechanics, such as calculating the energy levels for the electron in a hydrogen atom.

Feynman also had the opportunity to work with other established physicists. For example, he took a course from Manuel Vallarta, a Mexican physicist who was particularly interested in *cosmic rays.* Cosmic rays are actually high-energy particles. From Earth's point of view, they seem to come equally from all directions. This was puzzling to physicists. The stars in our galaxy (the Milky Way) are not distributed evenly through space. If cosmic rays came from stars in our galaxy, they would be expected to be unevenly distributed as well. Even if cosmic rays came from outside the galaxy, Vallarta believed that the magnetic field of the stars should scatter nearby cosmic rays so they would show an uneven pattern.

Vallarta asked Feynman to tackle this problem. Feynman used an interesting approach that he would employ later with subatomic particles: he ran the calculation in both directions—not only in toward Earth but also the path cosmic rays would take if they radiated out from Earth into deep space. Feynman showed that the stars' magnetic fields were not strong enough to affect the distribution of the cosmic rays. (It was later learned that some cosmic rays do come from within the galaxy, though the kind with the most energy come from outside.)

Vallarta was pleased with the work and offered to edit it and submit it to the prestigious *Physical Review* under both their names. Although Feynman had done most of the work, Vallarta explained that as the senior scientist his name should appear first. The paper duly appeared in the March 1, 1939, issue of *Physical Review* under the names "Vallarta and Feynman."

In 1946, however, Werner Heisenberg wrote a book on cosmic rays in which he discussed all the important papers in the field. At one point he discussed the possible influence of stellar magnetic fields on cosmic rays and noted that "such an effect is not expected according to Vallarta and Feynman." When Vallarta and Feynman next met, Vallarta acknowledged: "Yes, you're the last word in cosmic rays."

Inside Crystals

Feynman had essentially completed his graduation requirements in only three years, but MIT rules required that a student stay four years for a degree. Feynman did still have to write his senior thesis, which was expected to be a modest but genuine contribution to the field of physics.

John Slater served as Feynman's thesis adviser. Part of his job was to find a challenging but manageable problem for Feynman to tackle. Slater asked Feynman to find out why quartz crystals, when heated, expand much less than other substances such as metals.

Showing his typical desire to get to the essence of a problem, Feynman decided to first investigate the general problem of how atomic forces interact in crystals. Feynman found that this in turn depends on the distribution of electrical charges in the atomic nuclei and the surrounding "clouds" of electrons. Feynman combined electrostatics (a classical theory of electric charge) and quantum mechanics to create a relatively simple equation for calculating the atomic forces within a crystal.

Slater was pleased with Feynman's thesis, which appeared in *Physical Review* in 1939 with the title "Forces in Molecules." Because this approach was developed independently by another physicist, it became known as the Feynman-Hellman theorem. It has saved chemists thousands of hours of work in determining the behavior of atoms in *molecules* and particularly crystals.

Feynman was beginning to get noticed by the physics community. He would soon have the opportunity to work in the most exciting and perplexing part of physics: quantum theory.

Princeton and Quantum Mechanics

4

As graduation approached, Feynman had not thought much about where to go for his graduate studies. As quoted by Hapgood, when Feynman told one of his physics professors that he intended to go on to graduate study at MIT, the professor asked why. "Because MIT is the best school for science in the country," Feynman replied. "You think that?" the professor went on. "Yeah," replied Feynman. "That's why you should go to some other school," the professor finally replied.

Princeton was the logical choice—it was rapidly becoming the center for American theoretical physics, and most of the papers that Feynman and Welton had so eagerly read had "radiated" from that university. As Gleick notes, the top physicists at MIT, John Slater and Philip Morse, wrote to their Princeton colleagues, touting Feynman as having a "practically perfect" record and being "the best undergraduate student we have had in the physics department for five years at least." But there were two problems: Feynman had scored abysmally on the Graduate Record Examinations in history and English literature. Thus some people on the Princeton admissions committee thought Feynman was too "one-sided" to make a good adjustment to Princeton's more refined culture.

The second problem had nothing to do with physics or academics at all. H. D. Smyth, the head of the Princeton physics department, wrote to Morse:

> Is Feynman Jewish? We have no definite rules against Jews but have to keep their proportion in our department reasonably small because of the difficulty of placing them.

At the time, Jews were banned outright from many academic institutions. At "enlightened" places like Princeton they were admitted, but there was a quota. Evidently the admissions committee at Princeton felt that it had to discriminate against Jews at admission because of the discrimination the students would face later.

As Princeton continued to hesitate about Feynman's application, Slater and Morse continued to press his case. They assured Princeton that while Feynman was indeed Jewish, he was not arrogant and had an agreeable personality. (In other words, he did not fit the stereotype.) Eventually Feynman's obvious talent as a young physicist won out, and he was accepted to Princeton.

Feynman found a different social atmosphere at Princeton. MIT had been more casual, more working class (admittedly, a very select working class). Princeton was aristocratic, more like Britain's famous Oxford and Cambridge. Arriving in 1933, Einstein described Princeton in a letter (quoted by Gleick) as "A quaint ceremonious village of puny demigods on stilts."

Students went to tea in the afternoon and wore academic gowns to dinner. When Feynman first went to tea, the dean's wife, who was serving, asked him whether he wanted cream or lemon in his tea. "Both," blurted Feynman. Her reply would become the title of a book of Feynman stories: "Surely you are joking, Mr. Feynman."

Although Feynman struggled to adapt to the "high society" of Princeton, it was a different story in the classroom. Unlike MIT undergraduates, graduate students at Princeton were free to take whatever classes they wished, whether or not they were in their major. The only real requirement—a tough one—was to pass examinations and write and defend a thesis based on original research.

Feynman used his freedom to explore new areas of study. In particular, he began a lifelong interest in biology by taking a graduate course in that field.

Mentor and Friend

Soon after he arrived at Princeton, Feynman became a research assistant to John Wheeler. Although only seven years older than Feynman, Wheeler had worked for two years with Niels Bohr and was already one of the world's experts on nuclear physics and uranium in particular—a subject that would gain vast importance in the coming world war.

In appearance, the two men would seem poorly suited to collaborate. Feynman was younger, brasher, and already gaining a reputation as an eccentric genius. Wheeler, on the other hand, had already taken on the role of a respectable professor and dressed conservatively.

At their first meeting, Wheeler pulled out an expensive pocket watch and placed it on the table, implying that his time was valuable and would be parceled out exactly. Feynman took this all in and bought a cheap pocket watch. At their next meeting, when Wheeler put out his watch, Feynman took out his own timepiece and placed it next to Wheeler's. It was as though to say "my watch may be cheap, but my time is just as valuable as yours." Fortunately both men immediately saw the humor in the situation and burst out laughing. They soon became friends.

Feynman became Wheeler's teaching assistant in courses in mechanics and nuclear physics. When Wheeler needed to be absent, he put Feynman in charge of the class. Meanwhile, Wheeler and Feynman met once a week. At first Wheeler assigned research problems to Feynman, but it was not long before the relationship had changed from mentor and student to that of equal colleagues.

Feynman's work with Wheeler would be the heart of his development as a physicist. Feynman did not bother to go to most of the "advanced" physics courses, since he had already mastered the material. Wheeler offered him the chance to work on the same problems that were challenging the world's leading quantum physicists.

Equally important, this work gave Feynman the opportunity to "reinvent" quantum physics from the ground up. Just as Feynman always said that he needed to visualize to be able to understand and calculate, he also needed to work out theories by seeing how the pieces fit together. Sometimes this meant he would rediscover things that were already known, which some critics might consider a waste of time. For Feynman, however, this was the way to not just know how to do something but to have the kind of deep understanding that can in turn generate new ideas.

"Some New Ideas Are Needed"

At the end of his 1935 edition of *Fundamentals of Quantum Mechanics*, Dirac had noted that despite all that had been learned about the particle and wave theories of the electron, "it seems that some essential new physical ideas are here needed."

The idea needed was crucial for the fundamental understanding of matter. It had to do with how electrons as charged particles could exist at all.

To see how, begin with gravity, a more familiar force. As Newton found, the strength of the gravitational force exerted by an object is inversely proportional to the square of the distance from the object. For example, if an object is 100,000 miles from Earth it will experience a certain amount of gravitational pull from the planet. If the object moves to where it is only 50,000 miles away (half the distance), the force pulling it will be four times greater.

The electromagnetic force exerted by a charged particle such as an electron works similarly in that the force doubles each time the distance halves. However in electromagnetic terms, the electron is a "point charge"—it does not have a radius like the Earth does. While an object approaching the Earth will eventually hit the surface, there is no limit to how "close" one can get to an electron. The distance can keep diminishing, approaching zero. The result is that the field strength within the electron itself (the "self energy") would become infinite, which would also mean the electron has infinite mass (because of Einstein's $E = mc^2$). This is clearly nonsense in physical terms.

Pondering this puzzle in the summer of 1940, Feynman hit upon a typically bold idea: Since having an electron act on itself in this way causes so many problems, why not get rid of the electromagnetic field entirely? Instead, have electrons act directly on other electrons but not on themselves. The only problem, Feynman gradually realized, is that electrons do act on themselves, creating a kind of inertia called radiation resistance. (This explains the "extra" power that must be used to vibrate electrons to create an electromagnetic wave such as a radio or television signal.)

Feynman, Wheeler, and a Summer of Physics

Perplexed but still excited about his theory, Feynman went to Wheeler for help. It turned out that Wheeler had also been thinking about the alternative of using "action at a distance" rather than fields to explain the electron. However, when Feynman tried to explain radiation resistance by suggesting that after an electron acts on another electron, a returning force flows back from the other electron, Wheeler showed that this would not work. The problem is it would take time for the force to go from one electron to the other and back again, and it would take too long to account for the measured resistance.

Wheeler then added an intriguing idea of his own. It turns out that many kinds of equations in physics, including the classical wave equation, can be interpreted symmetrically with regard to time. The first, more normal way, has a wave moving outward from its source at the speed of light. The other, mathematically allowable but physically boggling, is to consider a wave moving toward its source but backward in time! (As strange as it sounds, such an approach is often necessary in quantum mechanics where mathematical possibility surprisingly mirrors physical reality.)

With this approach, the two waves (one out from the source electron and the other from the destination electron back to the source) take the same amount of time because the second wave travels as far backward in time as the time the first wave had taken to get to the destination.

Wheeler assigned Feynman the task of calculating this new theory of "retarded" and "advanced" waves. Feynman showed that the two waves would cancel each other out in just the right way to account for radiation resistance. Further, the wave and field equations could be dispensed with in favor of a simple, classical particle interaction across the distance.

As summer turned to autumn, Feynman and Wheeler eagerly extended their theory. Wheeler even suggested that all electrons and positrons (their positively charged counterparts) might be the same particle, traveling forward or backward in time. That idea, however, turned out to be *too* simple and had to be abandoned.

The Feynman-Wheeler Theory

In the spring of 1941 Wheeler asked Feynman to prepare and give a presentation on the new theories. The audience would contain many top-notch physicists including Wolfgang Pauli and Albert Einstein, many of whom might be critical of the theory and ask probing questions. Any graduate student, no matter how brash and how bright, would consider this to be a "high stakes" event. Indeed, in his memoir *Surely You're Joking,* Feynman described how his hands shook as he began to set up his notes for the talk.

> *But then a miracle occurred, as it has occurred again and again in my life, and it's very lucky for me: the moment I start to think about the physics, and have to concentrate on what I'm explaining, nothing else occupies my mind—I'm completely immune to being nervous. So after I started to go, I just didn't know who was in the room. I was only explaining this idea, that's all.*

After the talk, Pauli said that he doubted that the Feynman-Wheeler theory could be right. Einstein, however, said only that it would be difficult to apply this theory to gravity as well as electromagnetism. Nevertheless, Einstein did not say he thought the theory was wrong.

The next step was to generalize this theory to work with quantum mechanics as a whole. Wheeler made several attempts to do so but became bogged down, leaving the task to Feynman. (This work eventually became Feynman's doctoral thesis, though it [and a related paper written by Wheeler], were not published until 1945, after World War II.)

Feynman looked for a way to apply the "least action" principle he had learned as a youngster to the new world of quantum mechanics. (Recall that this principle allows one to determine the unique path or trajectory an object will take under specified conditions.) In spring 1941, Feynman learned of an obscure paper by Dirac suggesting a mathematical function for quantum mechanics that was "analogous" to the one used in classical (Newtonian) physics.

Analogous? Feynman hated imprecise language. He asked himself what "analogous" might mean. Feynman laid out the classical and quantum expressions side by side and found that by multiplying one by a constant value he could make them come out equal. This meant that the two systems were not just analogous, they were also proportional.

As summer approached, Feynman had the flash of insight that would lead to a revolutionary tool for quantum mechanics. He realized that the same mathematics Dirac had applied to waves could be used for working out the paths through space and time taken by subatomic particles as they interacted. It would allow him to sum up every possible path or "history." (Thus, this approach became known as "sum over histories" or *"path integrals."*). It had become a quite manageable calculus problem, although working out all the paths and the overall probabilities could be tedious.

Although much needed to be worked out, it was clear that Feynman, with Wheeler's help, had developed a third approach to quantum mechanics. Now there was Schrödinger's wave approach, Heisenberg's particle approach, and now Feynman's, based on the summing up of the action and possible paths taken by particles. All three approaches were successful (and indeed, mathematically equivalent). However, each contained a different understanding of the physics and had its particular practical advantages.

One day while Feynman was still working on this thesis, Wheeler visited Einstein and, according to John and Mary Gribbin, exclaimed to him that

> *Feynman has found a beautiful picture to understand the probability amplitude for a dynamical system to go from one specified configuration at one time to another specified configuration at a later time. He treats on a footing of absolute equality every conceivable history that leads from the initial state to the final one, no matter how crazy the motion in between. . . . This prescription reproduces all of standard quantum theory. How could one ever want a simpler way to see what quantum theory is all about!*

Meanwhile, however, a property of certain atomic nuclei had captured the attention of physicists and world leaders. The world would never be the same again.

Physics at War

5

By the end of the 1930s, a new world war was clearly looming. In 1939, Hitler's Germany conquered Poland and the next spring German tanks and planes were roaring deep into France. By 1941, Feynman, though still technically a graduate student, had been doing top-level quantum physics even as he worked to complete his doctorate, which he received in June 1942.

In normal times, the next step would be to get a position in research or teaching at a university. However, these were not normal times, and Feynman, like most college graduates of the time, did not know whether he would be in uniform in a few months or perhaps at work in a war-related industry.

Love and Crisis

Meanwhile, Feynman had found both love and tragedy in his personal life. During his time at MIT and Princeton, Feynman had overcome his shyness around girls, but his interest always seemed to turn back to Arline. Arline's direct approach to life impressed him, even though her cultured background often clashed with his rationalism and disdain for subjects such as philosophy that he considered to be undisciplined and muddled. Yet when Feynman seemed hesitant about doing something too unconventional, it was Arline who reminded him, "What do *you* care what other people think?" (This would become the title of a book of Feynman anecdotes.)

By 1942, Feynman and Arline had become engaged and tried to make future plans in face of the uncertainty of war. However, the day came when Arline found a strange lump on her neck and developed a cough that did not seem to want to go away. Sometimes it would be worse, other times better. Fevers would come and go. At first, doctors were puzzled, first diagnosing typhoid fever, a serious bacterial disease. (At the time there were virtually no antibiotics so the disease could only be allowed to run its course—many patients recovered.)

However, the course of Arline's symptoms did not really match up with typhoid. The next diagnosis was more ominous: Hodgkin's disease—a type of blood cancer that is often curable today but was fatal at the time. But Feynman found from his own hurried research that Hodgkin's was supposed to be a clear-cut diagnosis. Perhaps Arline's problem was something else?

The emotional roller coaster continued. Finally, there was a correct diagnosis. Arline had tuberculosis, another bacterial disease. This disease, sometimes called "consumption" or the "white plague," has a wide range of often perplexing symptoms. Most commonly, the disease starts in the lungs, bringing fever, chills, and coughing (sometimes including blood).

Like typhoid, there was no cure for tuberculosis until the development of effective antibiotics such as streptomycin during World War II. Rest and a warm, dry climate were recommended but could only postpone the inevitable.

Richard and Arline Feynman on the boardwalk at Atlantic City (AIP Emilio Segrè Visual Archives, Physics Today Collection; gift of Gweneth Feynman)

Despite the likelihood of only a few years together, Richard and Arline decided to marry. Feynman knew that his mother had serious misgivings about his marrying such a seriously ill young woman. Feeling a sense of urgency, they went to Staten Island and were married before a justice of the peace. There was no time for a honeymoon—as soon as they returned to the city, Arline was checked into a hospital in New Jersey. For Feynman, it was time to decide what to do about the war.

When Atoms Split

Ever since Rutherford had begun to bombard atoms earlier in the century, physicists knew that the nucleus or core of the atom held a tremendous amount of energy in terms of the force that bound it together. Early in the 1930s, the discovery of the neutron (an uncharged particle about the size of the proton) had led to the study of the forces holding protons and neutrons together in the nuclei of different types of atoms.

Physicists used newly invented particle accelerators such as the circular cyclotron to bombard atoms with protons. They discovered they could split a nucleus into two smaller nuclei. (Since the number of protons in a nucleus determines what element the atom belongs to, splitting it actually changes one element into another. This is "transmutation," long sought as a goal by the medieval alchemists.)

While the first experiments used light atoms such as lithium, attention soon turned to the heavy element uranium. The uranium nucleus was unstable (uranium is radioactive) and thus should be easy to split by getting it to absorb a neutron. Experiments by Otto Hahn and Fritz Strassman in early 1939, as interpreted by Lise Meitner, revealed that a uranium nucleus could be made to split virtually in two, with a tiny bit of mass being converted into a great deal of energy.

Further experimentation both in Europe and America showed that in addition to the two big "chunks" a nuclear *fission* also released two or more neutrons. What if these neutrons in turn hit nearby atoms?

Niels Bohr, arriving in the United States for a series of lectures, began to spread news of the German fission experiments to physicists such as Enrico Fermi and Leo Szilard. They performed their own fission experiments to confirm the results and were quick to see the implications of the newly discovered process. One day, as Szilard recalled to Richard Rhodes in *The Making of the Atomic Bomb*:

> *As the light changed to green and I crossed the street, it ... suddenly occurred to me that if we could find an element which is split by neutrons and which would emit two neutrons when it absorbs one neutron, such an element, if assembled in sufficiently large mass, could sustain a nuclear reaction.*

Szilard and Fermi proposed that a nuclear "pile" or reactor be designed. It would be fueled with uranium and use graphite to "moderate," or slow down, the neutrons enough for them to be effectively absorbed by the uranium atoms.

That August, Szilard, together with the physicists Edward Teller and Eugene P. Wigner, went to Albert Einstein at Princeton. (Einstein was a celebrity who had ready access to President Franklin Roosevelt.) They persuaded Einstein to write a letter to Roosevelt

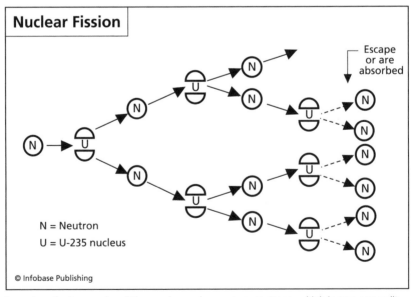

In nuclear fission, each splitting nucleus releases two neutrons, which in turn can split other nuclei. Properly arranged, this leads to a chain reaction.

Lise Meitner and Nuclear Fission

Throughout most of the 20th century, physics, like much of science, was dominated by men. An outstanding exception was Marie Curie (1867–1934), who received the Nobel Prize in physics in 1903 and the Nobel Prize in chemistry in 1911. Another woman physicist Lise Meitner (1878–1968) played an important role in the discovery of nuclear fission.

Meitner earned a doctoral degree in physics from the University of Vienna—"from" the university but not "at" it. At the time women were not allowed to attend lectures, so Meitner had to make special arrangements to do the required work. After getting her degree, Meitner went to the Max Planck Institute, one of the world's leading physics research institutions. (Planck allowed Meitner to attend his lectures, where women had never been permitted before.)

By 1909, Meitner was working with Otto Hahn on beta radiation (a form of energetic electrons). After World War I (where she helped operate X-ray equipment), Meitner, Hahn, and later Leo Szilard worked at the forefront of nuclear research, especially the possible creation of new heavy elements.

Unlike many other Jewish scientists, Meitner remained in Germany until 1938, when she finally made a harrowing escape from the Nazis. She then met with Hahn secretly in Denmark, where they planned further experiments in bombarding uranium atoms with neutrons. In trying to interpret the results of the experiments, a perplexed Hahn wrote to Meitner. Together with her nephew Otto Frisch, Meitner was able to explain how an atom could split, yielding lighter elements, accompanied by neutrons and a burst of energy. Meitner also made the key observation that the energy released corresponded exactly to the decrease in the total mass of the fission products. (This was in accordance with Einstein's famous equation $E = mc^2$.) Strongly opposed to any such weapons, Meitner played no part in the subsequent development of the atomic bomb.

In 1944, Hahn received the Nobel Prize in chemistry for his work with uranium, but Meitner's contribution to understanding fission was ignored. However, Meitner received the Max Planck Medal of the German Physics Society in 1946. In 1966, near the end of her life, Meitner, along with Hahn and Fritz Strassman, received the Enrico Fermi Award. In 1997, chemical element 109 was named meitnerium in her honor.

warning of the possibility of creating a bomb of unprecedented power and that German physicists might help Hitler obtain such a weapon. (In December, Werner Heisenberg did tell the German war department about the possibility of such a bomb. Fortunately, the Germans never developed a full-scale nuclear fission project.)

As a result of the Einstein-Szilard letter, President Roosevelt established the "Uranium Committee" to conduct fission research. (The British started a similar program, which was later combined with the American one.) At first the work was on a small scale and given a relatively low priority, but in summer 1942 the project was expanded vastly under the scientific leadership of the physicist Robert Oppenheimer. Code-named the Manhattan Project and put under the control of the U.S. Army Corps of Engineers, construction of three major facilities was soon under way. A huge plant at Oak Ridge, Tennessee, would separate the fissionable uranium-235 *isotope* from the much more common uranium-238 (which was also radioactive, but could not sustain a fission reaction). Simultaneously, at Hanford, Washington, nuclear reactors would be built in order to turn uranium into the highly fissionable and newly discovered element *plutonium.*

The third site, where the researchers would work and the bomb would be assembled and tested, was near Los Alamos, New Mexico. (It was hoped that the remote desert location, besides offering a measure of safety in case of a nuclear mishap, would also be far away from the prying eyes of spies or the news media.)

Off to the Secret City

Feynman first joined an army laboratory where he worked on a mechanical fire control (gun-aiming) computer. Meanwhile, the news about nuclear fission and its possibilities was percolating through the government and military establishment. When Feynman returned to Princeton to finish his doctoral thesis, Robert R. Wilson took him into his office and told him that he was forming a team of physicists to work on an atomic bomb.

Feynman, preoccupied with his thesis and disillusioned with war work, turned him down at first. He then thought about whether

Werner Heisenberg and the other physicists remaining in Germany might be working on such a bomb. That alarming possibility was enough to change Feynman's mind. Feynman signed up for what would become the Manhattan Project.

When Feynman arrived at Los Alamos in 1943, the secret installation was still a work in progress, swarming with construction workers and loads of equipment arriving by train. Los Alamos would be ruled by two strong-minded leaders, General Leslie Groves of the army and J. Robert Oppenheimer, a physicist from the University of California, Berkeley. Despite their different backgrounds, the rather conventional Groves and the rather flamboyant Oppenheimer had a knack for resolving their arguments with practical arrangements that kept the lab running relatively smoothly.

Oppenheimer knew and liked brash young physicists like Feynman. When Feynman told him about Arline's situation, Oppenheimer arranged for her to be moved to a sanatorium in Albuquerque. This meant that Feynman could visit her on weekends though it meant driving 100 miles over rough roads.

Feynman flourished in the tense but exciting atmosphere at Los Alamos. He soon gained a reputation as a resourceful problem solver. Oppenheimer noted in his journal that Feynman was "by all odds the most brilliant young physicist here, and everyone knows this."

The Human Computer

Feynman was assigned to the T or "theoretical" section of the lab, headed by Hans Bethe, the physicist whose papers had so impressed Feynman and Welton when they had begun to tackle nuclear physics as undergraduates. Specifically, Feynman and Welton were assigned to section T-4, which was in charge of calculating exactly how much fissionable material was necessary to trigger not a mere nuclear *chain reaction* but a full-fledged nuclear explosion—a *"supercritical mass."*

What Feynman contributed most was his talent for mathematical visualization, rapid, accurate calculation, and the imagination to find new ways to attack problems. He had a knack for solving complicated calculus problems when people with as much or more formal training did not know where to begin. The atom bomb project, with its need to predict the behavior of neutrons under rapidly changing conditions, had a tremendous appetite for calculation.

At the time there were no electronic computers (although several pioneering machines were in early stages of construction). To solve a complex problem required teams of clerks or mathematical assistants cranking away for hours on mechanical calculators. When these calculators, which looked a bit like overgrown typewriters filled with keys and gears, kept breaking down, Feynman took one apart and learned how to fix them. Given the urgency of the race to build the atomic bomb, there was no time to send the machines back to the factory to be repaired.

Feynman also realized that organizing the workers on the mathematical "assembly line" was as important as keeping the machines running. He learned the most efficient ways to break down complex problems into a series of steps that could be performed by the people—mostly scientists' wives—who worked the calculators. In essence, he created a series of recipes, or algorithms, for solving problems on a "computer" whose chips were human beings.

"The Puzzle of You"

Feynman's love of finding solutions to all sorts of puzzles showed itself in other ways. He wrote to Arline nearly every day. To keep up their spirits, Feynman and his wife sent each other elaborate puzzles. The first time they did this, a security officer blocked the letter because he thought it contained secret codes. After some argument, it was agreed that Feynman would provide a key to the message so the officer could decrypt it.

In one of his letters, Feynman admitted that he had probably become obsessed with the many locks that guarded the secret papers around the laboratories:

> . . . because I like puzzles so much. Each lock is just like a puzzle that you have to open without forcing it. But combination locks have me buffaloed. You do too, sometimes, but eventually I figure out you.

Soon Feynman mastered the combination locks as well. When people forgot the combinations to the safes containing their portion of atomic secrets, they came to Feynman. Feynman seemed to be able to get into any safe. Sometimes he could guess the combination or get it by trying some likely possibilities. (Some scientists liked to use numbers from their work, such as the values of *pi* or *e*. This guessing technique is still used to "crack" into computers today.)

Feynman learned that the safes could not distinguish between the correct number and one up to two places away, which cut down the number of combinations he had to try. He also learned to turn the knob until the bolt dropped, leaving the combination's last number.

Feynman's apparent disdain for security rules became widely known. One day he discovered a hole in the fence that would allow anyone to bypass the guarded gate and go in and out at will. To his surprise, Feynman discovered the guards had little interest in doing anything about the gap. To get the attention of the security officers, Feynman repeatedly checked in at the gate, went out through the hole, and came right back without having checked out. Eventually this earned a mild reprimand, but the hole got filled. (Ironically, for all the security efforts, there were two actual spies at the lab, a German refugee named Klaus Fuchs and an American Theodore Hall, who both were agents for the Soviet Union. The Soviets' espionage effort would give them a head start in developing their own atomic bomb a few years after the war.)

"Tickling the Dragon"

Meanwhile, the bomb project continued. America's largest industry was no longer automobiles or steel. It could be found at Oak Ridge, Tennessee, where they built thousands of centrifuges for magnetically extracting the uranium-235, the rare isotope (variety with a particular atomic weight) that could be made to split and explode.

But how could they assemble enough fissile (fissionable) material into the proper configuration? As recounted in *The Making of the Atom Bomb*, Otto Frisch noted that

> The idea was that the compound of uranium-235, which by then had arrived on the site, enough to make an explosive device, should indeed be assembled to make one, but leaving a big hole so that the central portion was missing; that would

allow enough neutrons to escape so that no chain reaction could develop. But the missing portion was to be made, ready to be dropped through the hole so that for a split second there was the condition for an atomic explosion, although only barely so.

When Feynman heard about this proposed experiment, he said that it would be like tickling the tail of a sleeping dragon. However this particular dragon would breathe radioactive fire!

The "dragon experiment" was set up at a remote site. A 10-foot iron frame called the "guillotine" surrounded blocks of uranium hydride. A "core slug" about two by six inches in size would be dropped down the central chute, accelerated by gravity. As it passed the core of the assembly, the assembly as a whole would form a *critical mass* for a fraction of a second. Because the uranium-235 was in a compound (hydride), it should not react nearly as violently as pure uranium. Still, it was not clear how theory would translate to reality . . . would it be a fission or fizzle, a modest surge of radiation, or a huge explosion?

Frisch noted the results:

It was as near as we could possibly go toward starting an atomic explosion without actually being blown up, and the results were most satisfactory. Everything happened exactly as it should. When the core was dropped through the hole we got a large burst of neutrons and a temperature rise of several degrees in that very short split second during which the chain reaction proceeded as a sort of stifled explosion.

Hedging Their Bets

Although the results of the dragon experiment were encouraging, there were still no guarantees the full-fledged bomb would work as predicted. They would hedge their bets. In Washington State, they built atomic reactors to bombard other uranium atoms to yield the artificial element plutonium, another material whose isotope 239 was fissile.

They would design two completely different types of bombs. One used uranium in two pieces, one of which was shot into the other like a shell in a gun. (This in essence would be like the dragon experiment, except that instead of the critical mass being momentary, it would exist long enough for a full nuclear explosion.)

The second design, using plutonium, was more sophisticated. Carefully shaped pieces of plutonium were made to come together or implode in a spherical shape, yielding the conditions needed for

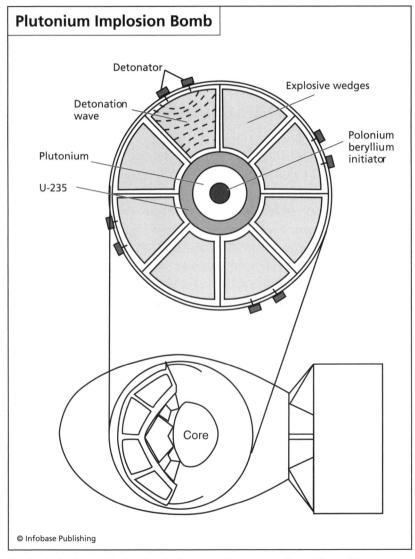

Plutonium Implosion Bomb

Detonator

Detonation wave

Explosive wedges

Plutonium

Polonium beryllium initiator

U-235

Core

© Infobase Publishing

The implosion-type plutonium bomb directs explosive waves inward toward the core.

the nuclear explosion. (The reason for using different materials and designs was simple—they could not know for sure that either would work, but using different principles increased their chances that at least one bomb would be ready in time for use in the war.)

Feynman did not contribute directly to the bomb design, but he did help with calculations necessary to determine how neutrons would behave under the conditions at the time the bomb would be set off. This involved many variables, including the mass of fissile material, as well as its shape and the shape of reflecting and absorbing materials.

Feynman made another important contribution that may have saved many lives and prevented the bomb project from being set back for months. Reports came from Oak Ridge that the highly fissionable enriched uranium was being stored in casks that were too close together. While this could not cause a nuclear explosion, it could lead to a deadly spray of radiation and perhaps a smaller explosion scattering the deadly material about the plant.

The core of the problem, Feynman realized, was that the workers handling the uranium had been told very little about what it was and how it might behave. Feynman went to Oak Ridge, gathered the workers together, and gave them an elementary talk about nuclear fission and the properties of uranium. This went against the grain of secrecy and the principle of telling each person only what he or she needed to know, but Feynman realized that people who understood the danger and how to avoid it would be highly motivated to do so. Here, as with the human "computers" back at Los Alamos, Feynman's ability to explain complicated processes and help people visualize them suggested the superb teacher he would become later in his career.

Saying Good-bye

In May 1945 Feynman had written to Arline:

> *The doc came around special to tell me of a mold growth, strep-tomycin, which really seems to cure TB in guinea pigs—it has been tried on humans—fair results except it is very dangerous as it plugs up the kidneys. . . . He says he thinks they may soon lick that—and if it works it will become available rapidly. . . .*

Keep hanging on tho—as I say there is always a chance some-thing will turn up. Nothing is certain. We lead a charmed life.

Unfortunately, powerful antibiotics such as streptomycin and penicillin would come too late for the Feynmans. In May 1945, with the first test of the nuclear bomb only about two months away, Arline's father told Feynman that his daughter was dying. Feynman borrowed a car from Fuchs (a friend and, unknown to Feynman, a spy). He made the long drive to Albuquerque that evening, having to repeatedly patch the car's worn tires along the way.

When Feynman arrived, Arline was too weak to talk, but he did his best to comfort her. She died a few hours later. Not able to face that reality, Feynman tried to lose himself in his laboratory work. Finally, Bethe insisted that Feynman go back to Far Rockaway for a break.

Angered because they would not accept his marriage with such a sick woman, Feynman had not visited or even communicated with his parents for almost three years. Their encounter now was painful and awkward, and Feynman spent much of his time walking on the beach he had known as a child.

Finally, though, a telegram arrived at the Feynman home. It was from Bethe, and it simply said "the baby is expected." Feynman knew what the coded message meant. As quickly as he could he made his way back to Los Alamos.

The Sun Rises Early

On July 16, 1945, in a remote spot in the New Mexico desert rather appropriately called Jornada del Muerto ("Journey of Death"), the first atom bomb, a plutonium implosion-type design, lay in a steel cradle suspended above the ground in a tower of girders. Scientists, some with grim humor, placed bets on the outcome of the test, rang-ing from a "fizzle" or dud to an out-of-control reaction that could blow away the Earth's atmosphere. (Admittedly, this last possibility was believed to be very unlikely.)

Lying down and looking through dark protective glass, Feynman and the other Los Alamos scientists waited in the predawn light as a series of thunderstorms repeatedly postponed the countdown. "And then, without a sound, the sun was shining, or so it looked," Otto Frisch would be quoted as saying in Gleick's book. In the same book, another physicist Isidor Rabi is quoted as saying of the light: "It blasted; it pounced; it bored its way into you. It was a vision which was seen with more than the eye." Then came a crack like a rifle shot, the rumble of thunder in the air, and finally the wind pushed ahead of the shock wave. The test, code-named Trinity, had been completely successful. The bomb had exploded with the force of 20,000 tons (18,143.7 metric tons) of TNT.

In the final official report on the test, what was seen in the surrounding countryside was described as follows:

> *The lighting effects beggared description. The whole country was lighted by a searing light with the intensity many times that of the midday sun. It was golden, purple, violet, gray, and blue. It lighted every peak, crevasse and ridge of the nearby mountain range with a clarity and beauty that cannot be described but must be seen to be imagined.*

The world's first atomic bomb is slowly raised into a 100-foot (30.5-m) tower for testing. (AP Images)

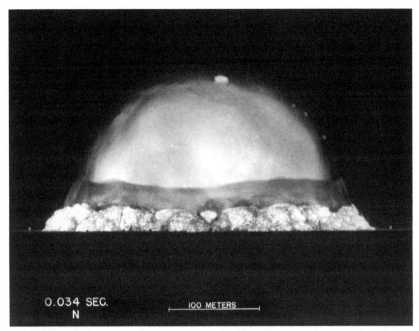

The successful test of the atomic bomb, code-named Trinity, took place near Alamogordo, New Mexico, on July 16, 1945. The photo shows the explosion 0.034 seconds after detonation. (Los Alamos National Laboratory Archives)

All the pent-up tension of many months seemed to dissipate with the fading of the mushroom cloud. Gleick quotes a letter of Feynman to his mother: "We jumped up and down, we screamed, we ran around slapping each other on the backs." It had worked! But the blazing flash of the bomb, "brighter than a thousand suns," made Robert Oppenheimer think of a description of the goddess Kali in the Hindu scriptures of India: "Now I am become death, the destroyer of worlds."

Feynman's time at Los Alamos had been one of excitement and shared purpose. Now that purpose had been fulfilled, but his life had become lonely and uncertain.

6

Writing the Atomic Playbook

Although it had been fear of Germany that had driven the atomic project, the Nazis had surrendered months before the successful bomb test. It was decided to use the bomb to try to force the surrender of Japan, which was fighting on bitterly despite having lost most of its navy, its resources, and even its cities (to firebombing).

On August 6, 1945, a uranium bomb nicknamed "Little Boy" was dropped on Hiroshima, Japan. Three days later a second bomb called "Fat Man," powered by plutonium, was dropped on another Japanese city, Nagasaki. Together, the two bombs killed about 150,000 people directly, with tens of thousands more to die later from burns, radiation sickness, and cancer. Japan surrendered a few days later, but the debate over the justification for the use of such terrible weapons continues to this day.

Physics Loses Its Innocence

For Feynman, as for many of the more thoughtful Manhattan project scientists, the prospects for the coming nuclear age looked grim. In a personal note quoted by Gleick, Feynman's words seemed bitter:

> *Most was known . . . Other people are not being hindered in the development of the bomb by any secrets we are keeping. They might be helped a little by mentioning which of two processes is found to be more efficient, & by our telling them what size parts to plan for—but soon they will be able to do to Columbus, Ohio, and hundreds of cities like it what we did to Hiroshima.*
>
> *And we scientists are clever—too clever—are you not satisfied? Is four square miles in one bomb not enough? Men are still thinking. Just tell us how big you want it!*

Edward Teller would soon be seeking people to work on what they called the "super"—the hydrogen fusion bomb, the one that would bring hydrogen atoms together and release 100 times the energy of the Hiroshima bomb. Feynman, though, wanted none of it. Fear of nuclear consequences as well as the pain of the loss of Arline combined to make him feel depressed, and he struggled to resume his civilian career after accepting a teaching post at Cornell University. As he recalled much later in his memoir *Surely You're Joking, Mr. Feynman:*

> *I returned to civilization shortly after that and went to Cornell to teach, and my first impression was a very strange one. I can't understand it any more, but I felt very strongly then. I sat in a restaurant in New York, for example, and I looked out at the buildings and I began to think, you know, about how much the radius of the Hiroshima bomb damage was and so forth . . . How far from here was 34th street? . . . All those buildings, all smashed—and so on. And I would see people building a bridge, or they'd be making a new road, and I thought, they're crazy, they just don't understand, they don't understand. Why are they making new things? It's so useless.*

Feynman went on to note that fortunately he and other scientists and engineers did continue "making new things." While the cold war would bring new crises, the feared nuclear war never came.

In October 1945, however, Feynman suffered another personal blow. He had finally had a long talk with his father, and they had reconciled, with his father expressing pride in his son's career. But Melville Feynman suffered a fatal stroke only a few days later. Feynman had lost the two people who had been most important to him.

Feynman had often found mental clarity in the process of writing his letters to Arline. He decided to write one final letter. As quoted by Gleick, it ended as follows:

> *My darling wife, I do adore you.*
> *I love my wife. My wife is dead.*
> *Rich.*
> *P.S. Please excuse my not mailing this—but*
> *I don't know your new address.*

He sealed the envelope. It would remain unopened until it was found in his papers after his death more than 40 years later.

Beginning an Academic Career

Feynman's spirits were raised by the number of prestigious universities offering him teaching positions. He was even offered a post at the Institute for Advanced Study at Princeton (where Einstein among others had settled).

However, Feynman had begun to doubt whether he still had the ability to do the kind of first-class physics a place like Princeton would expect. One afternoon, though, as quoted by Robert P. Crease in *The Second Creation*:

> *. . . while I was eating lunch, some kid threw up a plate in the cafeteria that had a blue medallion on [it]—the Cornell sign. And as he threw up the plate and it came down, it wobbled . . . And I wondered—it seemed to me that the blue thing [on the plate] went around faster than the wobble, and I wondered what the relation was between the two.*

This was hardly an earthshaking physics problem, but it intrigued Feynman and distracted him from his depression. Using some basic equations from Newton he determined that if the wobble was small, the blue thing went around exactly twice as fast as the wobble itself went around.

A bit pleased with himself, Feynman went to Hans Bethe and told him of his findings. Bethe was less than impressed, but later Feynman realized that the spin and wobble in the plate was analogous to something that mattered a lot more—the spin of an electron. Suddenly Feynman felt a surge of energy and returned to his prewar work in *quantum electrodynamics.*

It was this ability of Feynman's to make connections between seemingly unlike things that would leave a lasting impression on his colleagues at Cornell. In Gleick's biography one of them, the Polish-American mathematician Mark Kac, is quoted as giving this assessment of Feynman:

> *There are two kinds of geniuses: the 'ordinary' and the 'magicians.' An ordinary genius is a fellow whom you and I would be just as good as, if we were only many times better. There is no mystery as to how his mind works. Once we understand what they've done, we feel certain that we, too, could have done it. It is different with the magicians. Even after we understand what they have done it is completely dark. Richard Feynman is a magician of the highest caliber.*

A Shower of Particles

Magician or not, Feynman and other leading postwar physicists faced formidable challenges. Like Feynman, physics itself seemed to be catching its breath and struggling to find a comprehensive theory in which to fit the discoveries of the 1930s and 1940s. "The theory of elementary particles has reached an impasse," wrote the physicist Victor Weisskopf as quoted by Robert Crease. Weisskopf went on to explain that the mathematics used to describe particle interactions tended to spiral out of control, leading to infinite quantities. There was another problem: New particles were being discovered faster than researchers could fit them into current theory.

Starting in the 1930s, particle accelerators enabled physicists to create high-energy collisions that led to the discovery of many new particles. This is the 27-inch (68.6-cm) cyclotron at the radiation laboratory at the University of California, Berkeley, in 1934, with (pictured) M. Stanley Livingston (left) and Ernest O. Lawrence (right). (National Archives)

Back in the 1930s, physicists had begun building so-called atom smashers such as cyclotrons. They had also begun to take advantage of nature's own particle accelerator. Atomic nuclei zip into the Earth's atmosphere from space, the product of the Sun, far-off stellar explosions called novas and supernovas, and perhaps more mysterious sources. (These are the cosmic rays that Vallarta and Feynman studied in the 1930s.)

When these very energetic particles hit nuclei of atoms in the atmosphere, they produce showers containing a variety of particles.

These particles can be observed in a cloud chamber. This device expands gas (such as air with water vapor) by pulling out a piston. As the gas expands it cools, and a cloud forms around ions in the gas. Any particles coming through the chamber leave tracks in the cloud, something like the contrail of a jet airplane.

Analyzing such tracks led to some surprises. One of them, predicted by theory, was the positron, a particle that has the mass of an electron but with a positive rather than a negative charge. When a *photon* (light particle) with the right amount of energy hits a nucleus, its excess energy creates a pair of particles—an electron and a positron. This illustrated the way that mass and energy could be interchanged. Gradually it was discovered that each elementary particle had its twin, an antiparticle that had an opposite charge—or in the case of the uncharged neutron, an opposite spin.

In peering into the world within the nucleus where particles and energy turned into one another, physicists were now investigating

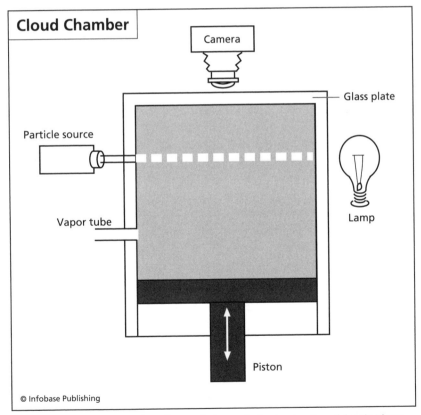

A cloud chamber creates a fog of vapor that reveals the tracks of particles that have passed through.

the actual forces within the atom. One, called the weak nuclear force, is what makes radioactive atoms decay (break down) and send out beta particles (high energy electrons or positrons). A question originally raised by Lise Meitner—whether beta particles come from the nucleus or the surrounding electrons, had been answered. A neutron in the nucleus becomes a proton plus an electron (the beta particle). But the mass of a proton plus an electron does not quite add up to that of a neutron. Enrico Fermi suggested that this missing mass was emitted in the form of a particle called a neutrino (Italian for "little neutral one").

Because the neutrino has no charge and almost no mass, it was very difficult to detect. By the 1950s, however, many nuclear reactors were in operation—and these were places where a lot of radioactive decay was going on all the time. Researchers set up a tank full of a solution of cadmium chloride and water. After shielding the tank with old battleship armor to keep out any other kinds of particles, they waited for a few neutrinos to hit hydrogen atoms in the water, ricochet, and eventually get captured by a cadmium nucleus. The nucleus in turn emits a gamma ray with a particular energy. The neutrino proved to be a very elusive beast: of the 10^{13} neutrons per square centimeter per second poured out by the nuclear reactor, only three per hour collided with atoms in the tank. But that was enough to confirm that they were there.

Neutrinos were the missing ingredient in the *weak force* of nuclear decay. Back in 1935, the Japanese physicist Hideki Yukawa had studied the *strong force*—the one that holds protons and neutrons together in the nucleus. He predicted that just as light has its energy carrier (the photon), the strong force would also manifest itself as a particle under certain conditions. Experimenters studying cosmic rays found such particles, which became known as *mesons* because they have a mass between that of the electron and that of the proton.

When a fast-moving proton from a cosmic ray or particle accelerator hits a proton at rest, the result can be two protons and a type of meson known as a neutral pi meson (or pion for short), a proton plus a positive pion, or if the energy is high enough, even two protons plus a whole flock of mesons. (Remember that under the right conditions more energy can be converted into more mass in the form of particles.)

With particles, antiparticles, photons, and an assortment of mesons, the possibilities for particle interactions were rapidly growing. Physicists needed a comprehensive way to describe what was going on.

The Shelter Island Conference

Starting in June 1947, Robert Oppenheimer held a series of conferences on behalf of the National Academy of Sciences. The first conference was to address "Problems of Quantum Mechanics and the Electron." However the meeting came to be known by its location on Shelter Island at the tip of Long Island, New York. In many ways this conference and its follow-ups would shape research in particle

The Shelter Island Conference in June 1947 allowed physicists to assess the many developments of the preceding two decades and to debate theories and methods in quantum mechanics. (AIP Emilio Segrè Visual Archives, Marshak Collection)

physics for the next generation. It was also Feynman's first opportunity to participate in a top-level physics conference.

The big concern at the conference was the failure of existing theories of quantum electrodynamics (QED) to be able to calculate the interaction of an electron in an *electromagnetic* field. As noted earlier, previous attempts had resulted in division by zero and infinite energy as one approached the electron's point of charge.

Meanwhile, two physicists, Willis Lamb and Robert Retherford, had probed hydrogen atoms using beams of microwaves. (Microwave technology had developed as an offshoot of radar research during the war.) Previous theory (developed by Dirac) suggested that at each rung of the "ladder" of possible energy states in the hydrogen atom, there were two states with equal energy. The results of the experiment, however, showed that there is actually a small but precise difference between each pair of energy levels. This result suggested that physicists should be able to find a way to avoid (or cancel out) the infinities and come up with finite numbers corresponding to the measured energy levels.

Hans Bethe had already made promising progress. Essentially, he calculated the energy of the electron as the previously found infinity *plus* a small correction corresponding to the force exerted by the hydrogen nucleus (which is a single proton). He then subtracted the energy of a free electron (one not bound to a nucleus), which is also infinite.

In effect it looked like this:

Infinity + "a little something" – Infinity = "another little something"

This process of canceling out infinities became known as renormalization.

Feynman's Funny Diagrams

As noted earlier, before he joined the atom bomb effort Feynman had come up with a promising new theory of particle interactions. It provided a way to calculate all the possible paths a particle could take, along with the probability of each path. This provided a complete picture of a given situation. Unlike Bethe's calculation, it also accounted for relativistic effects (such as the increase in mass of particles at speeds close to light as shown by Einstein at the beginning of the century).

Feynman now applied his theory to the electron. At first he could not get the infinities to cancel out, but then he got things to work properly. By now it was fall 1947 and the second in the series of conferences would be coming in April of the following year.

Even with his new method, Feynman found it difficult to keep track of the many different interactions and their related equations. Although he could not recall when it started, Feynman had begun to draw little pictures: a straight line for the electron component and a wiggly line for a photon. To show an interaction, he had the two lines meet at a point. According to Crease, Feynman did

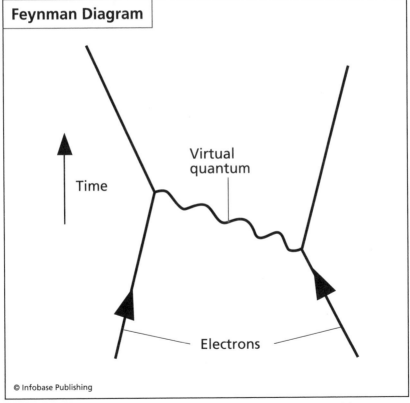

Feynman Diagram

Virtual quantum

Time

Electrons

A Feynman diagram showing two electrons repelling each other. The particles move upward as time passes. The virtual quantum carries the energy of repulsion.

remember that "at one particular stage, when I was still developing these ideas, making such pictures to help myself write the various terms—and noticing how *funny* they looked." Feynman even wondered if someday the *Physical Review* (the most prestigious journal in the field) might someday be "full of these odd-looking things." In fact, such diagrams would, in a decade or so, become a standard part of physics textbooks.

Feynman found the diagrams greatly aided his mathematical intuition. Soon he was able to look at a sequence of diagrams and determine without calculation whether the associated equations

Julian Schwinger: Noted American Theoretical Physicist

Julian Seymour Schwinger (1918–94) shared the 1965 Nobel Prize in physics with Richard Feynman and Sin-Itiro Tomonaga. Like Feynman, Schwinger grew up in New York, in a more urban setting than Feynman's Far Rockaway. He attended Columbia University, receiving a B.A. in 1936 and a Ph.D. in 1939. He then worked at the University of California, Berkeley, under Robert Oppenheimer.

Instead of going to Los Alamos like Feynman, Schwinger worked at the radiation laboratory at MIT, where he worked on physics connected with the development of radar—a vital wartime project.

After the war, Schwinger went to Purdue, where he taught until 1974. Using mathematical tools from his radar work, Schwinger tackled quantum field theory. He ended up developing the same basic approach as Feynman was developing independently, which eliminated the infinite quantities from the equations. Schwinger's work was more comprehensive mathematically than Feynman's, though perhaps harder to visualize. Schwinger was able to generalize the approach to deal not only with electrons but many other particles as well.

Schwinger's later work included the identification of separate types of neutrinos, one associated with electrons and another with their subatomic "cousins," muons. In the 1960s, he did fundamental work in the development of a theory embracing both electromagnetism and the weak nuclear force associated with radioactive decay. This work was further developed by Schwinger's student Sheldon Glasgow into the modern "electroweak" theory.

would converge (move toward a definite answer) or "blow up" into one of the dreaded infinities.

As Feynman discussed his new work with colleagues the reactions were mixed. For example Freeman J. Dyson recalled that

Thirty-one years ago [1949], Dick Feynman told me about his "sum over histories" version of quantum mechanics. "The electron does anything it likes," he said. "It just goes in any direction at any speed, forward or backward in time, however it likes, and then you add up the amplitudes and it gives you the wave-function." I said to him, "You're crazy." But he wasn't.

While Feynman was using his unique diagrams as an aid to calculation, Julian Schwinger developed a powerful but more conventional approach to quantum electrodynamics. (SPL/Photo Researchers, Inc.)

In his later years Schwinger defended controversial research on "cold" (low energy) nuclear fusion and resigned from the American Physical Society when it refused to publish his papers on the topic.

As with Feynman, one of Schwinger's most important legacies is as a teacher and mentor. He supervised the doctoral dissertations of more than 70 graduate students, four of whom went on to win Nobel Prizes.

Frustration in Pennsylvania

In 1948, a conference on "fundamental problems of theoretical physics" was held at Pocono Manor, Pennsylvania. Julian Schwinger, an American physicist of Feynman's generation, had worked out a comprehensive and thorough mathematical system for calculating the paths of particles while taking relativity into account.

After Schwinger finished his presentation, Feynman gave a rather hastily organized talk, in which he introduced his diagrams and the rules for using them. Among other things, he suggested that the positron could be treated as though it were an electron going backward in time. This startling notion probably contributed to the rather poor reception Feynman received. Bohr, in particular, thought Feynman was on the wrong track. To him, Feynman's methods looked something like cartoons or the kinds of trajectories that belong in Newtonian physics, not quantum theory. Ironically, one person who did understand Feynman was Schwinger, who saw that Feynman's approach was valid if not really to his own taste.

Feynman finally decided that most physicists simply weren't getting the point of his brief demonstrations. He would have to spell his approach out in a complete paper, step by step. By 1949, Feynman was able to give a much fuller presentation in the *Physical Review.* Later he remarked to his biographer Jagdish Mehra:

> *In private I had great amusement in thinking that my silly-looking diagrams, when published in the Physical Review, would poke fun at that august journal. I liked to think that my diagrams were the equivalent of sheep's livers and entrails into which the ancient Greek and Egyptian priests used to look for predicting the future.*

Although believers in an elegant, purely mathematical approach like Schwinger's scorned Feynman's diagrams at first, students and practical researchers quickly found that they were a practical aid. It was like having two ways to describe a football play. One way could use sets of numbers showing the velocity and momentum of the quarterback and wide receiver at each instant, plus that of the ball being passed from one to the other. The other way—Feynman's way—related the mathematics to a diagram a bit like that used by a football coach, with the Xs, Os, and arrows showing what each player is to do.

Doing quantum mechanics was a bit like looking at all the possible plays that could take place on the field and determining the likelihood of each. This turned out to be a lot easier when one had a good playbook, thanks to Feynman's work.

In "Wise Man," a book review that appeared in the October 20, 2005, edition of the *New York Review of Books,* Freeman Dyson summarized how Feynman's diagrams simplified the process of calculating complicated quantum processes:

> *If we want to calculate a quantum process, all we need to do is to draw stylized pictures of all the interactions that can happen, calculate a number corresponding to each picture by following some simple rules, and then add the numbers together. So a quantum process is just a bundle of pictures, each of them describing a possible way in which the process can happen.*

Writing more than 50 years after Feynman explained his thinking, Dyson notes:

> *Within twenty years after they were invented, these diagrams became the working language of particle physicists all over the world. It is difficult now to imagine how we used to think about fields and particles before we had this language.*

"Interesting Problems"

7

Although his work with quantum electrodynamics would have been achievement enough for any scientist, Feynman pursued a variety of research projects in the 1950s and 1960s.

Sunny Days in Brazil

Despite his success with quantum electrodynamics in the late 1940s, Feynman remained dissatisfied with his career. Cornell seemed to be too confining a place for the restless, still rather young, physicist. (The cold upstate New York winters did not help.)

One of Feynman's wartime colleagues Robert Bacher had established himself at Caltech near Pasadena, California—MIT's West Coast rival. He was soon expanding and modernizing the Caltech physics department. When Feynman made inquiries about going to Caltech, Bacher jumped at the chance to "land" one of physics' brightest new stars. Feynman would be on the Caltech faculty for the rest of his career, although this did not mean he would always be found on the Southern California campus.

As arrangements were being made for his move to Caltech, Feynman went still farther south, accepting an invitation to teach for six weeks at a physics center in Rio de Janeiro, Brazil. With typical enthusiasm and determination, Feynman arranged for a cram course in Portuguese so he could lecture to the Brazilian students in their native language.

As a teacher, though, Feynman was disturbed by the response of his Brazilian students. He discovered that while they were well prepared they stuck closely to the textbook. When Feynman tried to start a discussion on some topic not in the book or to give them the kind of challenging problems he loved to tackle, the Brazilian students did not respond. For the rest of his teaching career, Feynman fought against such rote learning, insisting that physics required imagination and the ability to apply knowledge in new

The campus of the California Institute of Technology (Caltech) in 1935. (California Institute of Technology, Archives)

ways. Despite these difficulties, Feynman would form strong bonds with Brazilian physicists and return repeatedly to lecture and work with them.

After enjoying Rio's sunshine and exotic nightlife, Feynman arranged to give a series of lectures at Caltech in January 1950. Several months later, he took his first trip to Europe, where he gave more lectures in Paris and Geneva, Switzerland. Feynman's whirlwind of traveling and teaching would continue for many years, thanks to Caltech's agreeing to offer him generous sabbaticals, or times off from his campus work.

A Brief Marriage

Feynman enjoyed the company of women and loved to flirt. However, he had steered clear of forming any serious relationships. In 1952, though, while touring a museum, Feynman recalled with fondness an art student named Mary Louise Bell whom he had dated back at Cornell. Abruptly, he wrote her a letter proposing marriage, and they were married in June 1952.

Unfortunately, Feynman and Bell had rather different ideas about how to live. Feynman's new wife tried to get him to dress and behave according to her idea of being professional. She had no interest in physics or physicists. In 1956, they agreed to divorce. At the time, divorce was not a no-fault affair—a reason had to be given to the judge. Bell told the court that Feynman played the bongos incessantly at home and did calculus problems in bed!

Liquid Helium and Other Puzzles

Some scientists find one great problem that will occupy them for their entire career, but Feynman was not like that. With the freedom Caltech provided him, he went from problem to problem. Typically, he would make a breakthrough, sketch out a theory, and leave the details to later researchers.

One of Feynman's more extended researches involved the boundary between the tiny world of quantum physics and the behavior of visible substances—in this case, liquid helium.

Helium is a gas familiar to many people as the stuff that goes into balloons or that, when breathed, gives one a squeaky voice. When helium gets very cold and becomes a liquid, however, it begins to behave very strangely. At a certain temperature the liquid flows without any friction at all—this is known as *superfluidity*. The liquid would seem to defy gravity, crawling up tubes and even going through holes that were too small to let helium gas through.

This behavior could not be explained by classical physics, but Feynman was able to apply the wave equations from quantum mechanics to show that the liquid helium was behaving as a "quantum fluid." Feynman used the same path integral methods he had successfully applied to electrons to calculate the behavior of the helium atoms.

Scientists had believed that at absolute zero (a temperature equal to about -460 degrees Fahrenheit, or zero on the Kelvin scale), all molecular motion stops. (Heat is nothing more than molecular motion, so this also means no colder temperature is possible.)

Feynman knew that in quantum mechanics, however, Heisenberg's uncertainty principle states that one cannot exactly determine both the position and velocity of any particle at the same time. Thus, even at absolute zero, some tiny but nonzero motion still had to exist. Based on this motion, Feynman was able to calculate the behavior of helium atoms that were only a few degrees warmer than absolute zero. By the 1960s, the full details had been worked out by other physicists.

Feynman also sought a quantum explanation for another strange phenomenon: *superconductivity*. This occurs in certain materials (usually at very low temperatures) where the material is able to conduct an electric current without any resistance (the electrical equivalent of friction). Under these circumstances, a battery can be connected to the superconducting material, allowing a current to flow. The battery can then be disconnected, and the current will continue to flow indefinitely.

Feynman hypothesized that subatomic particles that he called polarons were responsible for phenomena such as conductivity. He tried to explain superconductivity by using his familiar approach of building up the equations of motion with the aid of his diagrams.

This time Feynman was unsuccessful in his calculations, though he did develop some mathematics that was useful for the new field of solid-state physics, which would be vital for working with transistors and other new electronic devices.

The Office Next Door

Meanwhile, the frontier of quantum physics had moved from electrodynamics (explaining the behavior of the electron and other charged particles) to exploring the structure of the core or nucleus of the atom. Here, too, Feynman would play an important role, although the lead would be taken by a younger physicist in the office next door to him.

Murray Gell-Mann would become perhaps Feynman's closest colleague from the 1950s right up to Feynman's death in 1988. Gell-Mann had a background rather like Feynman's. He was Jewish, he grew up on New York's Upper West Side, and he was recognized early for his talent in science and mathematics.

In 1955, Gell-Mann came to Caltech, and he and Feynman were soon working together on fundamental problems of particle physics. By then, there was considerable interest in unraveling the true nature of the "weak force" that governs radioactive decay, where neutrons in certain atoms break down into several particles, such as a proton, an electron, and an antineutrino. Feynman and Gell-Mann came up with a theory to explain the weak force as being carried by particles called the W and Z bosons. (Another team of physicists, Robert Marshak and E. C. G. Sudarshan, also developed the theory and shared credit for it.)

In an article in *Discover* magazine, Susan Kruglinski quotes Gell-Mann's recollections of his first meeting with Feynman:

> *We had offices essentially next door to each other for 33 years. I was very, very enthusiastic about Feynman when I arrived at Caltech. He was very much taken with me, and I thought he was terrific. I got a huge kick out of working with him. He was funny, amusing, brilliant.*

The relationship would grow more strained as time passed:

. . . We argued all the time. When we were very friendly, we argued. And then later, when I was less enthusiastic about him, we argued also.

There is little doubt, though, that Feynman's arguments with his physics "neighbor" helped sharpen both of their thinking, helping to shape the development of the *Standard Model*—a unified explanation of atomic forces and interactions.

The End of Bachelor Life

Feynman's most important relationship in later life began when, while relaxing on a beach at Lake Geneva, Switzerland, he spied Gweneth Howarth, a 24-year-old Englishwoman working as an au pair. He quickly struck up a conversation with her. When she told Feynman that she was earning $25 a month, he offered to pay her $20 a week to become his housekeeper back at Caltech. Since she already had a pleasant place to stay and several boyfriends, Howarth at first was not inclined to accept Feynman's offer, though she enjoyed dating the older but still youthful-acting Feynman.

After Feynman returned to the United States, he and Gweneth continued to correspond. Finally, she agreed to take the housekeeping job, which was properly arranged through a third-party employer to avoid scandal.

When she arrived, Howarth found that Feynman's lifestyle took some getting used to. For example, Feynman had bought five identical sets of clothing (suit, shirt, and shoes), so he never had to decide what to wear! His attempts at cooking were rudimentary, and he usually ate out. Howarth's housekeeping skills soon made for a much more comfortable life.

Howarth maintained her independence. She had her own room and other boyfriends, although she dated Feynman as well. However, it gradually became clear that they were to be a couple. Feynman did not want to repeat his impulsive, disastrous marriage to Mary Lou Bell. He decided that he would set a date a few weeks away. If he still felt the same, he would propose to Gweneth. The time came and the answer was yes (although she made him wait until the next day for her reply). They were married on September 24, 1960.

Feynman and his three-year-old son, Carl, have an astronomy lesson outside their Altadena, California, home in 1965. They are looking for the comet Ikeya-Seki. (AP Images)

Third time turned out to be the charm. Their relationship would be dynamic enough to keep them both interested, yet stable at the core. Howarth shared Feynman's love of adventure and travel and maintained the spirit of independence he had admired so much in Arline. In 1962, they had a son, Carl, followed by a daughter, Michelle, in 1968. Both children later remembered a childhood filled with stories and puzzles.

Winning the Nobel Prize

In 1965, Feynman, Julian Schwinger, and the Japanese physicist Sin-Itiro Tomonaga were awarded the Nobel Prize in physics for their contributions to QED, or quantum electrodynamics. The news came in a 4:00 A.M. call from a correspondent for the American Broadcasting Company. At first, he did not want to believe the news, despite his phone ringing repeatedly with reporters seeking comment.

Feynman's reluctance to accept the news may have had something to do with the way in which the Nobel Prize is often seen as the culmination of a scientist's career. Generally by the time a scientist receives this highest of honors, his or her best work has been accomplished.

Feynman despised formality and ceremony, especially when royalty was involved. At first, he suggested he would actually refuse the prize, but his wife convinced him that doing that would give him even more publicity—and not good publicity at that. After going to Sweden, Feynman apparently had a change of heart. In this note found among his letters:

Feynman receiving the Nobel Prize in physics from King Gustaf VI Adolf of Sweden in Stockholm, December 1, 1965. (AP Images)

Reports of fathers turning excitedly with newspapers in hand to wives; of daughters running up and down the apartment house ringing neighbors' door bells with news; victorious cries of "I told you so" by those having no technical knowledge— their successful prediction being based on faith alone; from friends, from relatives, from students, from former teachers, from scientific colleagues, from total strangers. . . . The Prize was a signal to permit them to express, and me to learn about, their feelings. . . .

In his Nobel lecture, Feynman chose to focus not on the technical details of his work but on the process of discovery itself and how he learned even (or perhaps especially) from his mistakes.

After he won the Nobel Prize, many institutions wanted to give Feynman an honorary degree. Feynman always declined, as in this reply to the president of the University of Chicago:

. . . I remember the work I did to get a real degree at Princeton and the guys on the same platform receiving honorary degrees

Feynman dancing with his wife Gweneth at the Nobel ball in Stockholm, Sweden, on December 1, 1965. (AP Images)

without work. . . . It is like giving an "honorary electrician's license." I swore then that if by chance I was offered one I would not accept it. Now at last you have given me a chance to carry out my vow.*

Gradually, Feynman disentangled himself from media and well-wishers and began to focus again on his work. Having been so

Sin-Itiro Tomonaga: Influential Japanese Physicist

Sin-Itiro Tomonaga (1906–79) was a Japanese physicist who shared the 1965 Nobel Prize in physics with Richard Feynman and Julian Schwinger.

The second son of a Japanese philosopher, Tomonaga was born in Tokyo in 1906. He was an outstanding student at the Kyoto Imperial University. After graduate school, Tomonaga worked both in Japan and in Leipzig, Germany, where he was part of a research group led by Werner Heisenberg. With the outbreak of war, Tomonaga returned to Japan, where he finished the work on the study of nuclear materials for his doctoral degree. During this time he also studied the magnetron (a high-powered vacuum tube used for generating microwaves and radar waves).

In 1948, Tomonaga and his students began to pursue the same problems with infinite quantities that (unknown to them) were also challenging Feynman and Schwinger. Tomonaga discovered how to cancel out the infinities using a method similar to Schwinger's.

The following year Tomonaga accepted an invitation from Robert Oppenheimer to work at the Institute for Advanced Study at Princeton. Based on this work, Tomonaga proposed a model for how electrons and similar particles behave when pushed through very narrow (theoretically one-dimensional) conductors such as the carbon nanotubes being worked with today. (This is often called a Luttinger liquid, after codiscover Joaquin Luttinger.)

Today, there is considerable ongoing interest in exploring this and other phenomena of condensed matter physics. Possible applications include high-temperature superconductors and quantum wires made from carbon nanotubes. Such wires could conduct electricity 10 times better than copper at one-sixth the weight, which is of particular interest to NASA in its development of next-generation spacecraft.

successful with understanding electrons, he had come to the literal heart of the atom.

From Partons to Quarks

By the mid-1960s, physicists faced what became known as the particle zoo. By then they had found hundreds of particles, mostly had-

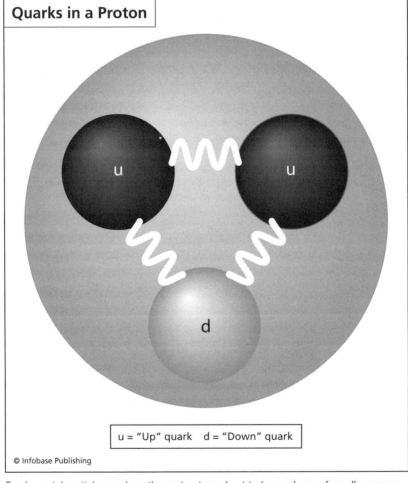

Quarks in a Proton

u = "Up" quark   d = "Down" quark

© Infobase Publishing

Fundamental particles such as the proton turned out to be made up of smaller components that Murray Gell-Mann called quarks. A proton, for example, consists of two up and one down quark.

Feynman talking with Murray Gell-Mann (left) at the seventh International Conference on High Energy Physics (also known as the Rochester Conference) in 1957. Gell-Mann's theory of quarks would describe how "families" of subatomic particles are constituted. (AIP Emilio Segrè Visual Archives, Marshak Collection)

rons (particles such as protons and neutrons that are subject to the strong nuclear force). The question was whether such particles were elementary, as are leptons such as the electron, or perhaps consisted of combinations of a few more basic particles.

Gell-Mann (and George Zweig, who was working independently) came up with such a model. Gell-Mann, who called these basic particles *quarks,* said that just three kinds of quarks (dubbed up, down, and strange) could provide the right combination of properties such as spin and electrical charge to account for all the known hadrons. (Later a fourth kind of quark, called charmed, was added.) We should note that these terms are simply labels: There is nothing particularly up or down about an up or down quark, for example, nor is a strange quark any stranger than the others.

Meanwhile, an experiment in 1968 at the Stanford Linear Accelerator Center (SLAC) confirmed that protons did have smaller objects inside. Feynman called these particles *partons* and for some time refused to agree that they were the same thing as Gell-Mann's quarks. Gradually, though, other experiments showed that the partons were up and down quarks, as well as confirming the existence of the other quark flavors. Gell-Mann later complained that Feynman had been unnecessarily stubborn in refusing to endorse the quark theory.

Feynman the Biologist

By the middle of the 20th century, the various fields of science had become highly specialized and largely isolated from one another. A physicist might focus on the fundamental nature of matter and energy and how they could emerge from the unimaginable heat of the big bang. A biologist, on the other hand, might be trying to understand how the raw and lifeless Earth of 4 billion years ago came to be filled with the most amazing variety of organisms, from simple bacteria to dinosaurs, whales, and people.

Naturally, each science took the discoveries of the others into account. Chemists have to be aware of atomic and molecular forces, while biologists spend much of their time on organic chemistry. But as science continued to develop at an explosive rate, it became increasingly rare for one person to make significant contributions in more than one field, such as in physics and biology.

By the mid-1960s, Feynman had become rather bored with physics. He and his colleagues were pretty much finished with quantum electrodynamics, while *quantum chromodynamics* (the study of quarks and other exotic particles) had been taken up by a later generation including his old colleague Murray Gell-Mann.

Meanwhile another Caltech physicist Max Delbrück had turned himself into a geneticist, and he was always trying to get physicists to tackle interesting problems in biochemistry. In summer 1960, Feynman had a sabbatical. He decided to accept Delbrück's invitation to work on the genetics of bacteriophages, viruses that infect bacteria. Feynman proceeded to master the basics of working in a biology lab and then learned how to count viruses and examine them for mutations.

This work was taking place less than 10 years after Watson and Crick had discovered the structure of DNA. It was clear that DNA carried or encoded the information passed from one generation of organism to the next. However, biologists did not yet know how the code was specified or how DNA instructions were used to build the protein building blocks of cells.

By painstakingly examining mutations and the resulting substances, Feynman was able to show that two separate mutations in the same gene (DNA sequence) could interact with each other or even suppress each other. (Feynman was urged to publish this discovery, but it was independently discovered and published elsewhere.) A year later, Francis Crick revealed the big picture of how mutations actually changed sequences in the DNA, rather like splicing a videotape.

Having mastered a considerable part of graduate biology, Feynman also volunteered to serve as a teaching assistant. Many biology students had trouble coping with mathematics, especially statistics, which had become an increasingly important part of their field. Feynman proved so successful in explaining mathematics concepts that he was voted the best teaching assistant of the year. Feynman later said to Mehra that [he] "got a tremendous boost by obtaining the best score of all teaching assistants; even in biology, not my field, I could explain things clearly, and I was rather proud of it."

Prophet of Nanotechnology

Feynman's exploration of the tiny world of the atom extended to a desire to find new ways to manipulate it. In 1959, Feynman gave a lecture at a meeting of the American Physical Society at Caltech. He titled it "There's Plenty of Room at the Bottom."

In this talk, Feynman suggested some amazing capabilities that could come as engineers worked at increasingly small scales. Molecules could be assembled mechanically (grasped using extremely tiny tools). Any desired substance that could exist chemically could thus be "made to order." Feynman was particularly interested in the

Nanotechnology Today

Feynman's ideas about tiny materials and machines did not attract much attention at first. For one thing, at the time Feynman gave his lecture the instruments needed to see and directly manipulate molecules and atoms were not available. However, starting in the 1980s, various types of scanning probe microscopes (SPM) were invented.

Although they sense different types of forces, the different kinds of SPM work in a similar way. A physical probe is moved back and forth, line by line, much as a computer scanner works. As the target substance interacts with the probe through electrical, magnetic, or molecular forces, the resulting physical stresses are converted to electricity by piezoelectric actuators. The data is then used to build up the image, which can then be processed further by a computer. Molecules and even individual atoms can be imaged.

In 1986, K. Eric Drexler, an American engineer and science writer, wrote a book entitled *Engines of Creation: The Coming Era of Nanotechnology.* ("Nano" refers to a nanometer, or one-billionth of a meter.) This book did more than anything else to popularize nanotechnology as a real possibility. In 1989, a journal called *Nanotechnology* began publication. The following year researchers succeeded in precisely arranging 35 xenon atoms. The resulting publicity encouraged people to find the 30-year-old Feynman article and to acknowledge its foresight.

Today, hundreds of products formed using some type of nanotechnology are being marketed. These include everything from sunscreen with titanium oxide, sticky "gecko tape" using a special form of carbon, new types of paints, and membranes that can turn salt water into drinking water.

The future may bring an exciting but alarming possibility. Nano-robotics involves the creation of "assemblers"—machines that can not only produce things but reproduce themselves. If successful, such machines would be the ultimate in automation: All one would have to do is provide the appropriate information and raw materials and let the machines do the rest. The cost of manufacturing would be dramatically reduced.

The alarming part is that the machines might get out of control, reproducing as fast as they can "eat" and consuming everything in their path. Eric called this ultimate result "gray goo"—matter reduced to its atoms. An organization called the Foresight Institute has been established to help nanotech researchers develop regulations to prevent the development of such voracious machines.

impact on computation. Computers could be made vastly more compact and powerful using tiny molecular circuits. (This was at a time when the first transistorized computers were just being built, and "chips" were more than a decade away.)

Data storage could also be revolutionized. Feynman calculated that if each bit of information could be represented by 100 precisely arranged atoms, all the information in all the books that had ever been written could be compressed into a cube about 1/200 of an inch wide (barely visible to the unaided eye).

Feynman even suggested that in the hospitals of the future a patient could swallow a pill-sized robot that could perform the most delicate surgery, even at the cell level. He believed that such miniature machines would be achieved one step at a time: build the smallest tools currently possible and control them using special sensors attached to the engineer's hands. Use those tools to build a set of still smaller tools, and so on. Eventually, the tools could be used to build tiny factories that could build still more factories, and so on.

Feynman pointed out a number of obstacles that would have to be overcome to achieve such applications. These included how to lubricate such tiny mechanical parts and how to deal with heat and electrical resistance. To encourage work in this field (which later became known as nanotechnology), Feynman offered two prizes of $1,000 each. The first was for building a tiny motor no larger than the specified dimensions. The second would go to the first person who was able to copy the information from the page of a book into a space shrunk to 1/25,000 of the original.

The prize for the motor was quickly won by someone who was able to use conventional tools but with superb craftsmanship. This was somewhat disappointing since it did not lead to any new technology. The "book" prize was won in 1985 by Tom Newman, a Stanford graduate student who succeeded in reducing the first paragraph of Dickens's *A Tale of Two Cities* to the required size.

Since 1993, the Foresight Nanotechnology Institute has given annual prizes, one each for theoretical and for experimental research in nanotechnology.

The Teacher
and the Performer

8

About 15 years after Feynman's death in 1988, his daughter Michelle was looking through the file cabinets at Caltech that contained her father's papers. Among technical papers and reports, she was surprised to find hundreds of letters that Feynman had written. As his colleague Freeman Dyson noted in a review of the collection of letters:

> *In these letters we see Feynman as a teacher. He spent much of his life teaching, and he threw himself into teaching as passionately as he threw himself into research. He wrote these letters because he wanted to help anyone who sincerely tried to understand. The letters that he preferred to answer were those which posed problems that he could explain in simple language. The problems were usually elementary,*

and Feynman's answers were pitched at a level that his correspondent could understand. He was not trying to be clever. His purpose was to be clear.

Feynman often answered letters that would have been ignored by most established physicists. Inevitably, someone would have some sort of universal theory that would surely revolutionize the understanding of gravity, the origin of the universe, or quantum mechanics. Feynman did not look down upon or make fun of such letters. Often he would point out something the writer had overlooked or ask for clarification.

Welcome to Physics

Feynman's most important contribution as a teacher came through the thousands of college students he introduced to modern physics. One of Feynman's favorite classes was "Physics X," which was intended for freshman and other beginners. There were no entrance requirements, no credit was offered, and anyone was welcome—provided they were willing to come at 5:00 P.M. on Friday afternoon. There was no set curriculum—Feynman would arrive, pick up a piece of chalk, and ask if there were any questions. The questions did not even have to be about physics. Sometimes, Feynman told stories about his safe-cracking days at Los Alamos.

In Peter Langston's Fun People Archive, Michael Scott, a student who later became the first CEO of Apple Computer, recalled one of Feynman's more dramatic demonstrations of basic physics:

There were 183 of us freshmen, and a bowling ball hanging from the three-story ceiling to just above the floor. Feynman walked in and, without a word, grabbed the ball and backed against the wall with the ball touching his nose. He let go, and the ball swung slowly 60 feet across the room and back—stopping naturally just short of crushing his face. Then he took the ball again, stepped forward, and said: "I wanted to show you that I believe in what I'm going to teach you over the next two years."

Feynman knew that the ball's return would stop short of his face because of the law of conservation of energy. The pendulum could not expend any more energy (or go any farther) coming back than it had going out. (Indeed friction and air resistance would cause a bit of energy to be lost.)

Scott later endowed a $1.5 million Richard P. Feynman Professorship at Caltech. He required that teaching ability be one of the main criteria in considering applicants for this post.

This story has a sequel. Another student, Matt Crawford, recalled that he took the same class some years later with another instructor in charge. When she did the bowling ball demonstration, it involved not a ball but a more massive sphere. She did not merely let go of the sphere: she gave it a bit of a push. Another professor, seeing this, quickly shoved her out of the way. A few moments later the pendulum came back, hitting the wall where the instructor's head had been! (The push, of course, had added energy to that already potentially stored in the pendulum, lengthening its path.)

The Value of Science

Following World War II, one of the concerns of many leading scientists was the lack of public understanding of how science worked and why it was uniquely valuable as a human endeavor. Too often science was seen as either the creator of wonderful new gadgets such as computers or satellites or as the bringer of possible catastrophe, as with the atomic bomb.

In a 1955 address to the National Academy of Sciences, Feynman spoke on "The Value of Science."

Scientists had made predictions of astounding accuracy—good enough by the 1960s to send a space capsule to the Moon and return it safely to Earth. People looked toward science as a source of exact and reliable answers. Feynman, however, saw science as being inevitably bound up with uncertainty:

> *The scientist has a lot of experience with ignorance and doubt and uncertainty, and this experience is of very great importance, I think. When a scientist doesn't know the answer to a problem, he is ignorant. When he has a hunch as*

to what the result is, he is uncertain. And when he is pretty damn sure of what the result is going to be, he is still in some doubt. We have found it of paramount importance that in order to progress, we must recognize our ignorance and leave room for doubt.

According to Feynman one problem with scientific knowledge is that nonscientists are not aware that not all science facts (let alone theories) are equally reliable:

Scientific knowledge is a body of statements of varying degrees of certainty—some most unsure, some nearly sure, but none absolutely certain. Now, we scientists are used to this, and we take it for granted that it is perfectly consistent to be unsure, that it is possible to live and not know. But I don't know whether everyone realizes this is true.

Feynman also believed that accepting the uncertainty of scientific knowledge means accepting the necessity of questioning authority:

Our freedom to doubt was born out of a struggle against authority in the early days of science. It was a very deep and strong struggle: permit us to question—to doubt—to not be sure. I think that it is important that we do not forget this struggle and thus perhaps lose what we have gained.

The Feynman Lectures

By the early 1960s, interest in science and technology in the United States had reached a new peak. In part this was a reaction to the Soviet launch of the *Sputnik* satellite in 1957 and the resulting space race.

Many teachers in university physics departments were concerned that their courses were scientifically outdated and unlikely to attract the interest of the young physicists of tomorrow. At Caltech, professors Robert Leighton and Matthew Sands approached Feynman and asked him if he would be willing to prepare a new series of introductory physics lectures.

Feynman agreed, although the project meant that he would have little time to pursue his research for several years. Indeed, he believed that giving a new generation access to the world of modern physics was vital. The resulting lectures, recorded in the mid-1960s, are still avidly read (or listened to on tape) four decades later.

For many people, science is a collection of rules and facts. In the introduction to the lectures, Feynman insists that

> ... things must be learned only to be unlearned again or, more likely, to be corrected.... The test of all knowledge is experiment. Experiment is the sole judge of scientific "truth."

Although experimentation is primary, Feynman notes that there are some important facts from which the scientific picture of the universe can be derived. Feynman says that if

> ... in some cataclysm, all scientific knowledge were to be destroyed, and only one sentence passed on to the next generation of creatures, what statement would contain the most information in the fewest words? I believe it is the atomic hypothesis (or atomic fact, or whatever you wish to call it) that all things are made of atoms—little particles that move around in perpetual motion, attracting each other when they are a little distance apart, but repelling upon being squeezed into one another. In that one sentence you will see an enormous amount of information about the world, if just a little imagination and thinking are applied.

Science for Poets

Another criticism of science is that it lacks feeling and cannot appreciate beauty the way poets or artists can. Feynman argues that

> Poets say science takes away from the beauty of the stars—mere globs of gas atoms. Nothing is "mere." I too can see the stars on a desert night, and feel them. But do I see less or more? The vastness of the heavens stretches my imagination—stuck on this carousel my little eye can catch one-million-year-old light. A vast pattern—of which I am a part ... What is the pattern or the meaning or the why? It does not do harm to the mystery to know a little more about it. For far more marvelous is the

truth than any artists of the past imagined it. Why do the poets of the present not speak of it?

For Feynman knowing how a rainbow is made, the refraction of light, makes the rainbow more beautiful. Put another way, understanding adds to experience rather than diminishing it. Further, Feynman also insisted that the scientist, like the poet, can "see the world in a grain of sand" or in a glass of wine. In *The New Quantum Universe* Feynman is quoted as saying that

> . . . it is true that if we look at a glass closely enough we see the entire universe. There are the things of physics: the twisting liquid which evaporates depending on the wind and weather, the reflections in the glass, and our imaginations adds the atoms. The glass is a distillation of the Earth's rocks, and in its composition we see the secret of the universe's age, and the evolution of the stars. What strange array of chemicals are there in the wine? How did they come to be? There are the ferments, the enzymes, the substrates, and the products. There in wine is found the great generalization: all life is fermentation. If our small minds, for some convenience, divide this glass of wine, this universe, into parts—physics, biology, geology, astronomy, psychology, and so on—remember that Nature does not know it! So let us put it all back together, not forgetting ultimately what it is for. Let it give us one more final pleasure: drink it and forget it all!

"Cargo Cult Science"

In his 1974 Caltech commencement address, Feynman referred to what he called "cargo cult science." An example of a cargo cult occurred during and after World War II in the Pacific. First the Japanese and later the Americans brought equipment and goods that were unfamiliar to the native peoples. These goods, often brought or dropped by air, included canned food, clothing, tents, tools, and weapons. During the war, natives (or their leaders) had some access to these goods. When the war ended the foreigners left and the flow of goods stopped.

Feynman lecturing at CERN, the European Organization for Nuclear Research, near Geneva, in 1965. (CERN/Photo Researchers, Inc.)

Some islanders reasoned that if they could recreate the activities of the foreigners they could restore their access to the much-desired goods. For example, they built replicas of airplanes out of straw, made "landing strips," and even control towers. The goods, of course, never came.

What does this have to do with science? Feynman compared "bad science" to cargo cultists. The first examples he gives are beliefs in UFOs, astrology, ESP, and other new age phenomena. After investigating many of these things personally, Feynman comes to the conclusion that not only do they not exist or do not work, believers ignore the lack of evidence while still insisting they are being scientific.

What is too often missing, Feynman suggested is:

> *... a kind of scientific integrity, a principle of scientific thought that corresponds to a kind of utter honesty—a kind of leaning over backwards... For example, if you're doing an experiment, you should report everything that you think might make it invalid—not only what you think is right about it ... Details that could throw doubt on your interpretation must be given, if you know them.*

Feynman then directs his criticism at a more mainstream field: education. Why, he asks, are there so many methods of teaching reading or mathematics, yet students' test scores never seem to go up? In general, Feynman said that "We ought to look into theories that don't work, and science that isn't science." Like the cargo cultists, "They follow all the apparent precepts and forms of scientific investigation, but they're missing something essential, because the planes don't land."

How can scientists avoid cargo cult science?

> *The first principle is that you must not fool yourself—and you are the easiest person to fool. So you have to be very careful about that. After you've not fooled yourself, it's easy not to fool other scientists. You just have to be honest in a conventional way after that.*

If science is to be a cooperative effort to find the truth, Feynman concludes that "the idea is to give all of the information to help others to judge the value of your contribution; not just the information that leads to judgment in one particular direction or another."

A War against Bad Textbooks

As his children began to learn mathematics in school, Feynman looked at the textbooks and teaching methods their school was using. He was dismayed to see that the curriculum seemed to consist mainly of a series of definitions that the students were expected to memorize. In his own work, he had always found that he needed to take an idea apart and put it back together in his own way before he truly understood it. As quoted by Gleick, Feynman's test for true understanding was the ability to do the following: "Without using the new word you have just learned, try to rephrase what you have just learned in your own language." As he had found in Brazil, distressingly few students seemed to be able to do this.

In March 1963, Feynman was appointed to the commission that selected school textbooks for use throughout the state of California. (Because of California's large textbook market, California's standards often determined the contents of textbooks used throughout the nation.) Most commission members relied on volunteer teachers or others to read the books and summarize them. Feynman, however, insisted he wanted to read the books himself. When he received a total of 300 pounds of books at his house, he had to change his plans. Nevertheless, he did spend many hours poring over the most important books, making notes, and often treating Gweneth to biting remarks about their lack of accuracy.

Feynman found that the mathematics books were filled with something called "the new math" that had become popular in the 1960s. Feynman did not disagree with the intent of the new math,

Overarching Principles

In 1964, Feynman gave the Messenger Lectures at Cornell University that were broadcast on television by the British Broadcasting Corporation (BBC) and appeared later in a book entitled *The Character of Physical Law.*

In the lectures, Feynman looks at one of the earliest yet most profound of the physical laws: gravitation. Using it as an example, he shows the general principles that seem to cut across all the realms of physics from the very large to the very small. Feynman focuses "not . . . on how clever we are to have found it all out, but on how clever nature is to pay attention to it."

The general principles Feynman discusses include conservation (maintaining an overall quantity despite changes in form, as with matter and energy) and *symmetry,* which is seen in the fact that physical interactions can be run either forward or backward (from the future to the past) without violating laws. It is only when one begins with matter that is ordered or organized that the overall state cannot be reversed (thus a broken egg or Humpty Dumpty cannot be put together again).

which was for students to learn to think about numbers rather than just memorize multiplication tables. However he found that the books spent too much time on ideas like sets and different number bases, rather than on the kind of mathematics concepts important to scientists.

The following year it was time to select science textbooks, and Feynman was equally dismayed with them. One book, for example, showed pictures of various machines and animals and asked what makes them move. The answer given was energy makes them move. To Feynman, this was worse than useless, since it merely used a label, energy, rather than saying anything at all about the sources of motion.

Educating the Public

In the 1960s and 1970s, many of the established institutions of society were being questioned and challenged by both young protesters

Feynman urged people who wanted a sense of the meaning and deep connections of physical law to try to understand at least some of the relevant mathematics:

> To those who do not know mathematics it is difficult to get across a real feeling as to the beauty, the deepest beauty, of nature. . . If you want to learn about nature, to appreciate nature, it is necessary to understand the language that she speaks in.

For Feynman, however, a robust imagination and a willingness to let nature "speak for itself" were also necessary for true scientific understanding. He noted that "our imagination is stretched to the utmost, not, as in fiction, to imagine things which are not really there, but just to comprehend those things which are there."

Feynman also warned students and colleagues:

> Do not keep saying to yourself, if you can possibly avoid it, "But how can it be like that?" because you will get "down the drain," into a blind alley from which nobody has yet escaped. Nobody knows how it can be like that.

and academic thinkers. Traditionally, however, scientists tended to avoid politics and social issues, even though the most critical issues increasingly involved the application of science and technology.

Having already experienced the consequences of the atomic bomb he had helped to build, Feynman had little patience for this point of view. He even wrote to the National Academy of Sciences and resigned his membership, saying that the organization was more concerned with its elite status than with advancing science and teaching the public about new developments.

Feynman the Performer

Ever since taking up the bongos during his time at Los Alamos, Feynman loved to perform and had a flair for the dramatic. He was always telling stories that had vivid punch lines, sometimes at his own expense. Years earlier, Feynman's friend and colleague Freeman Dyson had described him, according to Gleick, as "half genius and half buffoon [clown]." Later, however, this was revised to "all genius and all buffoon."

Feynman's showmanship rubbed some of his colleagues the wrong way. Speaking at a memorial service after Feynman's death, Murray Gell-Mann said that Feynman:

> surrounded himself with a cloud of myth, and he spent a great deal of time and energy generating anecdotes about himself. These were stories in which he had to come out, if possible, looking smarter than anyone else.

Feynman also enjoyed watching a good performance. He made an arrangement with James "The Amazing" Randi, a noted magician and debunker of so-called psychic phenomena. The deal was this: Randi could play tricks on Feynman at any time. Feynman in turn could ask any question he wanted about the trick, as long as it could be answered with a yes or no. As Randi recalled on Feynman Online:

> Some of [the tricks] took him a couple of days, some of them took him several months to figure out. He would sort of keep them in the back of his head, but he was so enormously curi-

ous about the whole world, of course, that this fascinated him entirely.

Feynman's endless curiosity about the world extended to its geography. Like many children of the time, the young Feynman had collected stamps, and this hobby often results in knowing a lot about obscure countries. In the 1970s, Feynman revived his interest in one of the most obscure, a Soviet Asian republic called Tannu Tuva. He and his friend Ralph Leighton became determined to visit that country.

To prepare, they learned the Tuvan language and even a bit about throat-singing, a unique vocal style that allows the singer to sing more than one note at the same time. However, as recounted in Leighton's book *Tuva or Bust!* their trip to Tuva was not to be: The Soviet government placed endless bureaucratic obstacles in their path. After Feynman's death, Leighton did visit Tuva and founded an organization called Friends of Tuva to educate people about the land's unique culture.

Feynman the Artist and Poet

The Feynman Online biographer Mark Martin notes that Feynman had felt the urge to artistic expression all his life, even while decrying what he saw as the pretentious nonsense of much modern art. Finally, Feynman took some beginning courses in drawing and painting. After some struggle to master the techniques, Feynman's work began to blossom, especially in his ability to sketch interesting portraits of people. As the online biography notes:

> *[Feynman] found that the lure of art lay, for him, in the personal satisfaction that his works could bring to others. He continued to practice art with physics for the rest of his life.*

As with art, Feynman had a somewhat difficult relationship with poetry, but sometimes could use the medium to good effect. In a 1955 address to the National Academy of Sciences on "The Value of Science," Feynman included the following poem:

Feynman also took an interest in art, though as with most things he did not follow the conventional approach. (© Shelly Gazin/CORBIS)

Deep in the sea,
all molecules repeat
the patterns of another
till complex new ones are formed.
They make others like themselves . . .
and a new dance starts.
Growing in size and complexity . . .
living things,
masses of atoms,
DNA, protein . . .
dancing a pattern ever more intricate.
Out of the cradle
onto dry land . . .
here it is standing . . .
atoms with consciousness
. . . matter with curiosity.

"Matter with curiosity" could almost sum up Feynman's many-faceted nature.

A Sampling of Feynman Stories

An extensive collection of stories by and about Richard Feynman is available in books such as *Surely You're Joking, Mr. Feynman* and from Web sites such as Feynman Online, from which the following example is taken:

Feynman and I would sometimes go camping together. On these occasions he would drive his van, which had Feynman diagrams painted all over it and a license plate that said Quantum. (Murray Gell-Mann had a license plate that said Quarks.) I asked Feynman if anyone ever recognized the diagrams. Yes. Once we were driving in the Midwest and we pulled into a McDonald's. Someone came up to me and asked me why I have Feynman diagrams all over my van. I replied, "Because I AM Feynman!" The young man went "Ahhhhh. . . ."

By the 1980s, Feynman had developed (some say cultivated) a reputation as a curious character—here, he is playing the bongo drums. (© Shelly Gazin/CORBIS)

Even Feynman sometimes seemed to tire of his reputation as an eccentric person. The speaker introducing Feynman for the Messenger Lectures at Cornell University in 1964 made a mention of Feynman's bongo playing. An irritated Feynman shot back:

On the infrequent occasions when I have been called upon in a formal place to play the bongo drums, the introducer never seems to find it necessary to mention that I also do theoretical physics.

A Final Challenge

9

In the late 1970s, when he was around the age of 60, Feynman was diagnosed with a rare cancer. A large tumor was successfully removed from his abdomen, but the tumor had already destroyed one of his kidneys and weakened him considerably.

In September 1981, doctors found that the abdominal tumor had returned with a vengeance, spreading and entangling his intestines. They tried to shrink the tumor with chemotherapy and then radiation, but to little effect. Finally the surgeons operated for more than 14 hours. When Feynman's aorta (the main artery leading to the heart) unexpectedly split, the surgeons fought to control the bleeding. A call went out for blood donors, and the response from Caltech students and staff and engineers at the nearby Jet Propulsion Laboratory was immediate. Finally, Feynman was stabilized and faced a long, slow recovery.

(Opposite page) *In a regular computer, a set of bits can only represent one number at a time. In a quantum computer, states are superimposed so that the same set of bits here can represent both 4 and 5.*

As he had when Arline had become ill, Feynman diligently did his own medical research, seeking possible treatments that the doctors might have missed. But Feynman and his doctors soon agreed that Feynman probably had only a handful of years left.

By fall 1982, Feynman began to return to teaching and research. There would still be time for him to make an important contribution to one of today's most important fields: computer science.

Feynman and Computer Science

Since the beginning of electronic computing, Feynman had a strong interest in the development of faster and more capable machines.

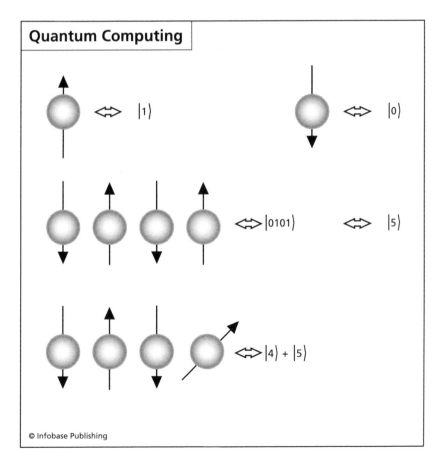

After all, he and his colleagues had struggled during the war with calculating the physics of nuclear explosions armed with nothing more than mechanical calculators. Feynman was particularly interested in designing computers that could run the simulations needed to understand the problems of particle physics.

Feynman's interest in modern computers was spurred when the computer scientist Ed Fredkin visited Caltech in 1974. Fredkin was working on designing a new kind of "reversible" computer. By this he meant a computer that could run all operations either forward or backward. While this might not sound like a useful thing to do, it turns out that all calculations in quantum mechanics are reversible—they can go forward or backward in time with equal validity.

Quantum Computing

In 1982, Feynman gave the keynote speech at an MIT conference on computing. It included an astonishing proposal:

> Can you [simulate quantum mechanics] with a new kind of computer—a quantum computer? It's not a Turing machine, but a machine of a different kind.

By "Turing machine" Feynman meant a conventional computer of the kind first envisioned in the 1930s by the British mathematician Alan Turing. In such a computer, such as the kind found on most people's desks, a given memory location can only contain one value at a time. (For example, it might have the binary digits 11001100 or 11001101, but not both at the same time.)

Drawing on quantum mechanics, Feynman suggested a new form of computer memory. As the experiments with light waves and particles had shown, until an observation (measurement) is made, there are many potential states particles can be in. If atoms are brought into a suitable relationship called coherence, it should be possible to store many numbers in the same memory location. If an operation such as multiplication is applied to this "quantum bit" or "qubit," all the stored numbers could be multiplied simultaneously.

There are many possible applications for the potentially infinite computational power of a quantum computer. These include simulation of complex physical processes, which was Feynman's main

Fredkin needed to learn more about quantum mechanics, and he was in the right place. Fredkin and Feynman made a deal: Fredkin would teach Feynman computer science and Feynman would return the favor by teaching Fredkin quantum mechanics. However, as Fredkin was quoted later in *The New Quantum Universe,* the relationship was sometimes strained:

> *It was very hard to teach Feynman something ... what Feynman always wanted was to be told a few hints as to what the problem was and then to figure it out for himself. When you tried to save him time by just telling him what he needed to know, he got angry because you would be depriving him of the satisfaction of learning for himself.*

interest in such machines. However, a more troubling possibility has emerged today with the development of the cryptography that protects everything from state secrets to credit card numbers. Modern cryptography depends essentially on multiplying very long prime numbers—numbers that cannot be divided evenly. "Cracking" such codes can be made almost impossible if the numbers used are long enough.

With a quantum computer, however, the toughest of today's codes could be broken in a matter of seconds, using an algorithm (mathematical recipe) that has already been designed.

The codes remain safe for now. Quantum computers have been built, but they consist of only a few qubits. There are many practical problems with designing a reliable quantum computer. The main problem is that the qubits are quite unstable. They tend to "decohere," or break down from many stored numbers to a single one. (This is like the wave function collapsing when a particle is observed.) This means that any attempt to retrieve data from the quantum computer may cause it to collapse.

Nevertheless, scientists are making some progress toward developing useful quantum computers. One approach is to store the same data using a large number of molecules. Thus when one or a few molecules are "read" to get the data, the data would remain stored in the rest of the molecules.

The Connection Machine

In the early 1980s, even as he was struggling with life-threatening illness, Feynman made another contact with the computer world. Feynman's son was a computer science major. The younger Feynman began to work with another undergraduate, Daniel Hillis, who was proposing a new kind of very fast computer. In "Richard Feynman and the Connection Machine," Hillis recalls

> *One day when I was having lunch with Richard Feynman, I mentioned to him that I was planning to start a company to build a parallel computer with a million processors. His reaction was unequivocal: "That is positively the dopiest idea I ever heard."*

However, Hillis continued:

> *For Richard a crazy idea was an opportunity to either prove it wrong or prove it right. Either way, he was interested. By the end of lunch he had agreed to spend the summer working at the company.*

The new computer was called a connection machine because the million processors were to be connected by a communications network that would parcel out the data for the calculation, coordinate the processing, and collect the results.

Hillis and his colleagues were able to raise a few million dollars and rent an old mansion outside of Boston. They were still arguing over the details of the business when their recruit stepped in the door, saluted, and said "Richard Feynman reporting for duty. OK, boss, what's my assignment?"

Hillis and his staff of MIT almost-graduates were rather taken aback. Hillis had not thought about what Feynman's actual role with the company would be. They decided that Feynman would be asked to advise them on the application of *parallel* processing to scientific problems.

Feynman was not impressed. "That sounds like a bunch of baloney," he replied. "Give me something real to do."

To gain time, they sent Feynman out to buy office supplies. They then thought about the implementation of the machine, and

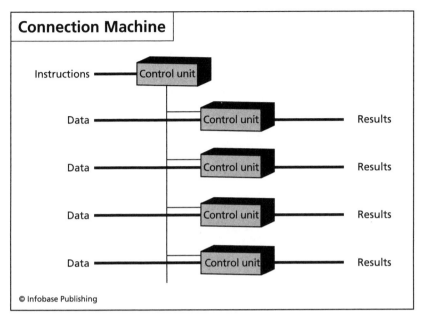

Connection Machine

Instructions ——— Control unit

Data ——————— Control unit ——————— Results

Data ——————— Control unit ——————— Results

Data ——————— Control unit ——————— Results

Data ——————— Control unit ——————— Results

© Infobase Publishing

Seeking a way to harness computers to do calculations for quantum mechanics, Feynman helped computer scientist Daniel Hillis develop the connection machine. Unlike a typical computer with one or more processors, the machine breaks down calculations into hundreds of bits of data that are operated on by thousands of processors and then reassembled.

they decided that the communications network was the most critical part. While the individual processors were actually quite simple, the machine that would connect them—the router—was not. It was not practical to connect each processor to every other one—the number of wires required would be greater than astronomical. Instead, each processor would be connected to 20 others in what Hillis described as a "20-dimensional hypercube." The problem was that there would often be more messages flitting about than there were wires available. The router would have to figure out whether there was a path available for each message. If not, the message would have to be held in a storage area, or buffer, until a path became free.

Feynman began to study the diagrams for the router circuit. Although the computer science students could explain how the network was supposed to work, Feynman, as usual, preferred to start with an open mind. He looked at the network as a physical structure and used pencil and paper to simulate how each circuit worked, gaining a "bottom-up" understanding of the whole.

Feynman spent most of his time studying the circuits, but he also pitched in on other tasks. He helped wire the computer room, set up the machine shop, doing the kinds of tasks he no doubt remembered from the hectic days of the Manhattan Project.

Meanwhile, the design of the machine continued. They decided they had better start with a more manageable number of "only" 64,000 processors. As for the circuits, they were not the kind of thing one could just order out of a catalog. Integrated circuits had to be designed, along with the necessary packages and connectors. There also had to be cooling mechanisms that could cope with the considerable amount of heat that would be generated by all those closely packed components. New kinds of programming languages and software tools were also needed. (Most existing programs were designed to do things "serially"—first one thing, then the next. The new computer would do many things in parallel, or at the same time.)

Another challenge was managing a team of people with different specialties and points of view. Here Feynman proved the value of his experience at Los Alamos. He told them that they should pick one experienced person in each field, such as electronics, packaging, or software. That person would become a team leader, and the leaders would coordinate with each other.

Another of Feynman's contributions came from his extensive contacts in the scientific community. He sought out people who were working on interesting projects that needed high-powered computing and invited them to come and tell the group about their work.

Feynman did not forget his original assignment. After completing his study and simulation of the communications circuits, he concluded that the machine would need five buffers to manage its data. Hillis and the other computer scientists disagreed: They said it would need seven buffers and decided to go with that number.

In spring 1984, they ran into a snag in manufacturing the processor chips. They were just a bit too large for the manufacturing equipment to handle. The only way to make them small enough was to cut off two buffers from each chip, reducing the total from seven to five. Fortunately Feynman had been right all along—five would be enough!

Feynman continued consulting with the Thinking Machines company for about five years, working on various problems. These included his writing a program to do quantum chromodynamics

Computers with "Brains"

One important application for computers like the connection machine is the building of neural networks. Conventional programmers begin with algorithms or "recipes" for such tasks as computing or sorting data. They write precise and exhaustive instructions. For example, suppose one is writing a program to correctly identify the shapes of letters in an image, in order to convert them to text. A conventional program might have a whole set of rules that would be checked in order to tell the difference, for example, between a "b" and a "d."

Although people often think of the human brain as being like a computer, the brain actually works quite differently. In computers, the main memory is "random access," meaning that the processor can move or fetch data to or from any arbitrary location. In the brain, each location or neuron is physically connected to anywhere up to several hundred other neurons. Instead of there being a central processor, there are networks of neurons, sometimes working together to form even larger networks.

While such networks can be simulated on conventional computers with the aid of the appropriate software, parallel processing computers such as the connection machine turned out to be ideally suited for neural networks. Each of the 64,000 processors could form up to 20 connections or "associations" with other processors.

Instead of writing a specific program to solve a problem, a neural network program is given a goal (such as recognizing letters) and allowed to randomly try a variety of procedures. Where a connection leads to a successful result, its value or "weight" is increased. Gradually the network "learns" to solve the problem without more than occasional tweaks by the programmer.

Neural networks have become particularly adept in such tasks as character and even face recognition, "data mining" (finding patterns in data), and even identifying suspicious credit card transactions. Another big advantage of neural networks is that they can often adjust successfully to changes in their environment.

(QCD), adding up all the possible path vectors for particles much as he had done in the 1940s—only millions of times faster!

Challenger

On the morning of January 28, 1986, the space shuttle *Challenger* lifted off from Pad 39B at Cape Kennedy, Florida. The crew would include the first nonastronaut, a teacher named Christa McAuliffe. She was scheduled to broadcast several programs from space, to be beamed into thousands of classrooms.

It had been unusually cold the past several days, and the liftoff had already been postponed twice out of concern that the temperature might affect seals called *O-rings* that covered the joints in pipes in the solid rocket booster (SRB). Nevertheless, the "Go" was finally given, and the huge rocket slowly rose into the early morning sky.

However, just as the rocket lifted off, an O-ring failed, spewing hot gas. The gas in turn burned through the attachment to the external fuel tank, which then blew apart, sending pieces of the rocket and shuttle pinwheeling through the sky. The shuttle's crew cabin remained intact, plunging into the sea. All seven crew members died.

President Ronald Reagan announced a high-level investigation into the causes of the accident. A few days later, Feynman received a call from the head of NASA (and one of Feynman's former students), William Graham, asking him to serve on the investigative committee.

When Feynman was asked to serve on the *Challenger* commission he was reluctant. His health was failing rapidly, and he was concerned whether he could live long enough to complete the assignment. However, Gweneth urged him to take the job, as quoted in *So What Do You Care What Other People Think?*

> *If you don't do it, there will be twelve people, all in a group, going around from place to place together. But if you join the commission, there will be eleven people—all in a group, going around from place to place together—while the twelfth one runs around all over the place, checking all kinds of unusual things. . . . There isn't anyone else who can do that like you can.*

Feynman relented. He told the commission that they could have six months—but only six months—of his full-time attention. He then had JPL engineers give him a thorough briefing on every significant aspect of the shuttle's engines.

William Rogers, the chairman of the commission, seemed to move at a leisurely pace in scheduling meetings. Feynman, who knew he had little time, objected. Rogers in turn was worried that Feynman would be an uncontrollable maverick who would disrupt the process and prevent the committee from coming to a unanimous and acceptable conclusion. Finally Rogers compromised with Feynman and allowed him to interview some NASA engineers on his own.

Another commission member, General Donald J. Kutnya, had a question about the possible effect of cold on O-rings—a concern raised by an astronaut who had to remain secret to protect his career. Suspicion had fallen on the O-rings following the discovery of an image of the liftoff showing black smoke and then flame coming out of an area of the shuttle near the main fuel tank.

No one seemed to know, however, just how the cold might have caused the O-rings to fail. Feynman decided to conduct an experiment. The next day there was a televised public portion of the hearing, and Feynman came prepared. He slipped a sample of the O-ring material into a clamp and plunged it into one of the Styrofoam cups of ice water routinely provided at such meetings.

When cued by the general, Feynman switched on his microphone and announced the following:

> *I took this stuff I got out of your [O-ring] seal and I put it in ice water, and I discovered that when you put some pressure on it for a while and then undo it it doesn't stretch back. It stays the same dimension. In other words, for a few seconds at least, and more seconds than that, there is no resilience in this particular material when it is at a temperature of 32 degrees. I believe that has some significance for our problem.*

At first the media seemed oblivious to the significance of what Feynman had done, but they eventually caught on. It turned out that NASA had fatally ignored a bit of simple physics and material science.

Feynman testifies before the Rogers Commission investigating the Challenger *space shuttle disaster. With a simple demonstration involving an O-ring and a glass of ice water, Feynman reveals the fateful flaw.* (© Bettmann/CORBIS)

Feynman found that the problems at NASA went far deeper. Requests from engineers for data on the safety of the O-rings at cold temperatures had been ignored by NASA officials. Further, there seemed to be a pervasive lack of concern about safety. Early in the shuttle program, NASA had proclaimed that the odds of a flight-ending disaster were at least many thousands to one, but gave no real basis for the calculation.

Feynman and later statisticians placed the odds closer to 100 to 1. And in 2003 a second shuttle, *Columbia,* burned and broke up in the atmosphere because its protective heat-resistant tiles had been damaged on takeoff.

Feynman wanted his conclusions about the safety included in the main body of the report, but Rogers disagreed. They compromised: Feynman's report appeared as Appendix F in the *Rogers Commission* report. Feynman literally had the last word: "For a successful technology, reality must take precedence over public relations, for Nature cannot be fooled."

Final Days

Feynman's service on the Rogers Commission would be his last major achievement. In February 1988, he was back in the hospital with a ruptured gastrointestinal ulcer and then his remaining kidney failed. Feynman knew his body was failing fast, and he decided not to try to gain a few months more of life by going on kidney dialysis. His biographer James Gleick says that:

> *Shortly before midnight on February 15, 1988, his body gasped for air that the oxygen tube could not provide, and his space in the world closed. An imprint remained: what he knew, how he knew.*

His last reported words were typical Feynman: "I'd hate to die twice. It's so boring."

Conclusion:
Assessing a Life

Feynman's pivotal role in the development of modern quantum physics cannot be denied. Together with Schwinger and Tomonaga, Feynman established a comprehensive theory of the interaction between light and particles, particularly the electron. He went on to make significant contributions to what became the theory of quarks, or quantum chromodynamics. Feynman also made important contributions to the study of super fluidity, superconductivity, and solid-state physics.

Feynman left an equally important legacy to physics in the mathematical method of "path integrals" that, together with his Feynman diagrams, allow researchers to manage the layers of calculations needed to plot all sorts of quantum interactions. In recent years cosmologists such as Stephen Hawking and later *string* theorists have been able to use Feynman's methods to chart the history and structure of the universe itself.

Feynman's core contributions to physics alone would make him one of the most important scientists of the 20th century. However, he also bequeathed ideas such as nanotechnology and quantum computing that today form the basis for emerging industries.

Any assessment of Richard Feynman must also include his considerable cultural impact. In a 2005 article for the *New York Review of Books,* Freeman Dyson wrote that Feynman had become a "public icon," along with Albert Einstein and Stephen Hawking. Dyson observed that

> *Scientists who become icons must not only be geniuses but also performers, playing to the crowd and enjoying public acclaim. Einstein and Feynman both grumbled about the newspaper and radio reporters who invaded their privacy, but both gave the reporters what the public wanted, sharp and witty remarks that would make good headlines. Hawking in his unique way also enjoys the public adulation that his triumph over physical obstacles has earned for him. . . . Einstein, Hawking, and Feynman shared an ability to break through the barriers that separated them from ordinary people. The public responded to them because they were regular guys, jokers as well as geniuses.*

Dyson also noted that the great icons have another quality: a deep and enduring wisdom:

> *Feynman was also a wise human being whose answers to serious questions made sense. To me and to hundreds of other students who came to him for advice, he spoke truth. Like Einstein and Hawking, he had come through times of great suffering, nursing Arline through her illness and watching her die, and emerged stronger. Behind his enormous zest and enjoyment of life was an awareness of tragedy, a knowledge that our time on earth is short and precarious.*

Perhaps the last word should be left to Feynman himself. In 2005, Feynman's sister Joan edited a collection of Feynman's letters

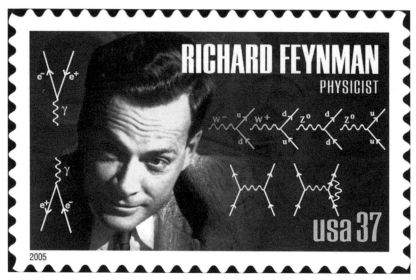

In 2005 the U.S. Postal Service issued a stamp honoring Richard Feynman as part of a set dealing with great American scientists. (AP Images)

with the title *Perfectly Reasonable Deviations from the Beaten Track.* "I was born not knowing and have had only a little time to change that here and there," Feynman said in a letter written to Armando Garcia in 1985.

As a postscript, on May 5, 2005, the U.S. Postal Service issued a set of four commemorative stamps honoring American scientists. One of them was Richard Feynman, who appears surrounded by eight tiny Feynman diagrams.

CHRONOLOGY

1896   Henri Becquerel discovers radioactivity in uranium.

1897   The electron is the first subatomic particle to be discovered (by Joseph Thomson).

1900   Max Planck uses the idea of a "package" of energy (a quantum) to explain radiation.

1905   Albert Einstein uses the quantum theory to explain the photoelectric effect.

1911   Ernest Rutherford describes the atom as being like a miniature solar system—a nucleus with electrons orbiting around it.

1913   Niels Bohr introduces the quantum theory of atomic structure.

1918   *May 11* Richard Feynman is born in Far Rockaway, New York.

1919   Rutherford demonstrates that an atom of one element can be bombarded and transformed into an atom of a different element.

1925   Werner Heisenberg, Max Born, and Pascual Jordan develop a theory of quantum mechanics based on particle interactions.

1926   Erwin Schrödinger develops an alternative approach to quantum mechanics based on waves.

1932   James Chadwick discovers the neutron.

1939   Lise Meitner and Otto Frisch publish a paper on nuclear fission.

World War II begins in Europe.

Albert Einstein warns President Franklin Roosevelt about the possibility of nuclear weapons.

1941   *December 7* Japan attacks Pearl Harbor; United States enters the war against Germany three days later.

1942   *June* Feynman receives his Ph.D.

July Feynman marries Arline Greenbaum.

August The Manhattan Project begins to develop an atomic bomb.

Scientists in Chicago create the first self-sustaining nuclear chain reaction.

1943   Feynman goes to Los Alamos, New Mexico, to work on the Manhattan Project.

1945   Arline Feynman dies of tuberculosis.

Atomic bombs are dropped on the Japanese cities of Hiroshima and Nagasaki.

Feynman begins his academic career teaching physics at Cornell University.

1948   Feynman introduces what come to be known as Feynman diagrams to visualize particle interactions.

1950 Turning down an offer from the prestigious Institute for Advanced Study at Princeton, Feynman goes to Caltech, where he will spend the rest of his career.

1953 Feynman publishes a paper on the behavior of liquid helium.

1954 Feynman receives the Albert Einstein Award.

1959 Feynman "invents" nanotechnology (microscopic machines) in a talk called "There's Room at the Bottom."

1960 *September 24* Feynman marries Gweneth Howarth— they will have a son, Carl, and a daughter, Michelle.

1963 Feynman's popular undergraduate physics lectures begin to come out in book form.

1964 Murray Gell-Mann and George Zweig use the term *quark* to describe the ultimate fundamental particles.

1965 *October 21* Richard Feynman, Julian Schwinger, and Sin-Itiro Tomonaga share the Nobel Prize in physics for the development of quantum electrodynamics.

1969 Feynman proposes the existence of "partons" to explain the results of high-energy particle collisions. The term would later be used to refer to both quarks and gluons.

1974 At 1974's Caltech commencement address, Feynman warns students that they need to think rigorously and avoid "cargo cult science."

1981 Superstring theory is introduced; Feynman approaches it with some skepticism.

1985 The first connection machine, a "massively parallel" computer is produced by Daniel Hillis with help in design and analysis from Richard Feynman.

A first book of Feynman anecdotes, *Surely You're Joking Mr. Feynman,* is published.

1986   In a dramatic hearing before Congress, Feynman demonstrates what caused the *Challenger* space shuttle disaster.

1988   *February 15* Feynman dies in Los Angeles, California.

What Do You Care What Other People Think?, Feynman's second collection of stories, is published.

2005   *May 4* The United States Postal Service issues a stamp commemorating Richard Feynman, as part of a set of American scientists.

GLOSSARY

atom   the smallest unit of a chemical element, consisting of a nucleus surrounded by electrons

black body   an object that absorbs all wavelengths of light and thus appears to be black

chain reaction   the result of neutrons from one atomic fission hitting nearby nuclei and triggering more fissions that release still more neutrons

Challenger   the NASA space shuttle that broke up shortly after liftoff on January 28, 1986

classical mechanics   the laws of motion worked out by Isaac Newton, which give accurate results except for very small or very fast objects

cosmic rays   these are actually high energy particles, not rays, that travel throughout space

critical mass   the amount and arrangement of material necessary to create a nuclear chain reaction

electromagnetic force   the force between charged particles, such as protons and electrons

electromagnetic waves   vibrations of electromagnetic energy that move through space, such as light waves and X-rays

electron   a fundamental particle; it is negatively charged and orbits the nucleus of an atom

element   a basic substance (such as oxygen) that cannot be chemically broken down into simpler substances

fission   the process by which a neutron hits a heavy nucleus (such as uranium), splitting it into two pieces and releasing energy

inertia   the tendency of a moving object to keep moving and a stationary object to remain fixed, unless acted upon by some outside force

ion   an atom or molecule that has more electrons than protons (or vice versa); for example, an atom that loses an electron (which is negatively charged) gains a net positive charge and becomes a positive ion

isotope   a variety of an element that has a particular atomic weight

least action   the principle that a moving object will always take the path involving the shortest distance and least time

meson   one of many kinds of particles that consist of a quark/anti-quark pair held together by gluons

molecule   a combination of atoms held together by chemical bonds

nanotechnology   direct engineering of materials on the scale of individual atoms or molecules

neutron   an uncharged particle about the size of a proton; it helps hold the nucleus together

O-ring   a donut-shaped seal designed to be flexible yet maintain its integrity under stress; failure of an O-ring caused the *Challenger* disaster

parallel computer   a computer that uses multiple processors that work simultaneously on the same problem

parton   hypothetical particle that Feynman proposed to be part of the inner structure of subatomic particles; the term would later be used to refer to both gluons and quarks

path integrals   the mathematical method devised by Feynman to "sum up" the possible paths of particles and eliminate troublesome infinities

photon   a particle of light

plutonium   an artificial element that is radioactive and can be used for nuclear fission

proton   a positively charged particle in the nucleus of atoms; the number of protons determines the chemical element

quantum   a fixed unit of energy that can be absorbed or emitted as part of particle interactions

quantum chromodynamics (QCD)   the theory that explains the interaction of components within the atom, especially quarks

quantum electrodynamics (QED)   the theory that explains how particles interact with each other and with electromagnetic fields

quark   one of six fundamental particles whose combinations make up most other kinds of particles

radioactivity   particles or energy sent out from atoms that spontaneously break down

relativity   Einstein's theory that space, time, mass, and energy are interrelated; it explains the behavior of objects traveling near the speed of light

Rogers Commission   congressional panel that investigated the *Challenger* disaster

Standard Model   the accepted theory that describes the "families" of particles and their component quarks

string theory   a theory that replaces fundamental particles with infinitesimal vibrating "strings" that form loops

strong force   the force that holds together particles in the nucleus of an atom

superconductivity   the property of some materials (usually at very low temperatures) that allows an electrical current to flow indefinitely

supercritical mass   the amount and arrangement of fissionable material needed to create a nuclear explosion

superfluidity   a property of certain very cold substances such as liquid helium, allowing it to flow in surprising ways, such as up the side of a flask

symmetry   an arrangement that does not change when some operation (such as flipping or rotation) is applied

uranium   a naturally occurring radioactive element; one isotope, uranium 235, is susceptible to nuclear fission

wave model   treatment of light, electrons, and other particles as acting like waves, subject to wave equations

weak force   the force responsible for radioactive decay

FURTHER RESOURCES

Books

Brown, Laurie M., and John S. Rigden. *Most of the Good Stuff: Memories of Richard Feynman.* New York: American Institute of Physics, 1993.

> *A fascinating collection in which Feynman's eminent colleagues including Murray Gell-Mann, John Wheeler, Freeman Dyson, and Julian Schwinger tell stories about their interactions with Feynman and explain the significance of his work.*

Crease, Robert P. *The Second Creation: Makers of the Revolution in Twentieth Century Physics.* Piscataway, N.J.: Rutgers University Press, 1996.

> *Describes the competing theories of particle physics out of which emerged the modern "standard model" of particle interactions. Provides good context for Feynman's work and its relation to that of other physicists.*

Feynman, Richard. *The Art of Richard Feynman: Images by a Curious Character.* Basel, Switzerland: GB Science Publishers, 1995.

> *Although Feynman was not an artist in the conventional sense, he was interested in art and approached it in his usual unique way. This volume includes Feynman's writings about drawing and art, as well as some of his drawings.*

———. *The Character of Physical Law.* New York: Modern Library, 1994.

> *In this lecture Feynman looks at selected physical laws and explains the methods and properties they have in common. Feynman celebrates the elegance and simplicity of natural laws and the remarkable fact that nature works this way.*

———. *Classic Feynman: All the Adventures of a Curious Character.* New York: W. W. Norton, 2006.

> *A treasury of Feynman anecdotes. Includes the previously published* Surely You're Joking, Mr. Feynman *and* What Do You

Care What Other People Think? *plus new material and a CD of a Feynman lecture.*

————. *The Meaning of It All: Thoughts of a Citizen Scientist.* New York: Basic Books, 2005.

A series of lectures Feynman originally gave in 1963, exploring questions that are still vital today, including the role of uncertainty in science and the conflict between science and religion.

————. *Perfectly Reasonable Deviations from the Beaten Track: The Letters of Richard Feynman.* New York: Basic Books, 2005.

Edited by Feynman's daughter, Michelle, this volume collects four decades of Feynman's letters. His correspondents include not only other famous scientists but also students, fans, and ordinary people. The letters are often intimate and reveal many facets of Feynman's personality.

————. *The Pleasure of Finding Things Out: The Best Short Works of Richard P. Feynman.* New York: Basic Books, 1999.

Presents a variety of previously unpublished or hard to find short writings by Feynman, including interviews, popular science writings, and his Nobel Prize acceptance speech.

————. *QED: The Strange Theory of Light and Matter.* Princeton, N.J.: Princeton University Press, 1985.

Using accessible language and his trademark wit, Feynman explains quantum electrodynamics (QED), the theory that explains the interaction between light and charged particles.

————. *Six Easy Pieces: Essentials of Physics, Explained by Its Most Brilliant Teacher.* New York: Basic Books, 2005.

Collects the more elementary parts of the celebrated Feynman Lectures on Physics including the relationship of physics to the other sciences.

————. *Six Not-So-Easy Pieces: Einstein's Relativity, Symmetry, and Space-Time.* New York: Basic Books, 2005.

A sequel to Six Easy Pieces that tackles somewhat more difficult concepts in physics, offering clear explanations.

Gleick, James. *Genius: The Life and Science of Richard Feynman.* New York: Vintage Books, 1991.

An acclaimed science writer paints a vivid portrait of Feynman, his complex personality, life, times, and achievements.

Gribbin, John, and Mary Gribbin. *Richard Feynman: A Life in Science.* New York: Plume Penguin, 1998.

> *The strength of this biography is in its explanation of the often difficult concepts needed to understand the significance of Feynman's work and its place in the overall development of modern physics.*

Hapgood, Fred. *Up the Infinite Corridor: MIT and the Technical Imagination.* Reading, Mass.: Addison-Wesley, 1993.

> *Tells the story of one of America's leading engineering schools and its unique culture, from early 20th-century dynamos to computer hackers and nanotechnology. Much of this culture was in its formative period while Feynman was there as an undergraduate.*

Hey, Anthony J. G. *Feynman and Computation: Exploring the Limits of Computation.* Cambridge, Mass.: Westview Press, 2002.

> *Combines concepts from Feynman's lectures on computation with personal reminiscences. Topics include nanotechnology, computer chip design, and physical simulation.*

Hey, Tony, and Patrick Walters. *The New Quantum Universe.* Rev. ed. New York: Cambridge University Press, 2003.

> *A lively survey of the development of quantum mechanics in theory and applications. This provides a larger context for understanding the significance of Feynman's work.*

Leighton, Ralph. *Tuva or Bust! Richard Feynman's Last Journey.* New York: W. W. Norton, 1999.

> *A moving memoir in which Leighton describes his friend Richard Feynman's interest in a remote Siberian republic and how they began the difficult task of planning a trip there. Unfortunately Feynman died before the bureaucratic and other obstacles could be overcome.*

Mehra, Jagdish. *The Beat of a Different Drum: The Life and Science of Richard Feynman.* New York: Oxford University Press, 1994.

> *An extensive biography that is rich in stories about Feynman's personal life as well as tracing the development of his scientific work in considerable detail. In addition to interviewing Feynman toward the end of his life, the author interviewed many of the physicist's friends and colleagues.*

Parnell, Peter. *QED: A Play by Peter Parnell; Inspired by the Writings of Richard Feynman and Ralph Leighton's* Tuva or Bust! Milwaukee, Wisc.: Applause Theater & Cinema Books, 2002.

Script of a stage play inspired by anecdotes and adventures from Feynman's life.

Rhodes, Richard. *The Making of the Atomic Bomb.* New York: Touchstone, 1988.

A lengthy but lively account of the development of the atomic bomb, from key discoveries in nuclear physics to the experiments at Los Alamos.

Video and Audio

Feynman, Richard. "Bits and Pieces of Richard's Life and Times." SoundPhotosynthesis.com. Video Cassette #V90-88.

Includes a variety of Feynman's memorable activities including playing the drums, conducting workshops, and testifying at the Challenger hearings.

———. "The Character of Physical Law." Excerpt from Messenger Lectures at Cornell University. [video]. Available online. URL: http://www.youtube.com/watch?v=pRkNu049oyM.

Feynman explores the meaning of past and future in physics. Surprisingly, most if not all physical laws look the same when run forward or backward.

———. "Computers from the Inside Out." SoundPhotosynthesis.com. Audio Cassette #A29-85 and videocassette #V23-85.

Feynman offers his unique take and pioneering ideas about computer design and the use of computers in science.

———. "Idiosyncratic Thinking Workshop." SoundPhotoSynthesis.com. 5 audio cassettes #A30-85 and video cassette V441-85.l.

Offers the essence of two five-day workshops held by Feynman about creative thinking in science and in life.

———. "The Very Best of the Feynman Lectures." New York: Basic Books, 2005. 6 CDs.

Digitally mastered excerpts of the lectures on topics ranging from basic Newtonian physics to relativity and quantum mechanics.

Infinity, starring Patricia Arquette, Dori Brenner. First Look Pictures, 1996.

A movie about the relationship between Richard Feynman and Arline Greenbaum, centered on her illness and his work on the Manhattan Project. DVD, released in 2002.

Internet Resources

"Basic Feynman." Available online. URL: http://www.basicfeynman.com/. Accessed February 12, 2009.

Provides links to books, audio, video, quotes, and other information about Feynman.

"The Best Mind Since Einstein." WGBH.org. Available online. URL: http://shop.wgbh.org/product/show/7620. Accessed December 7, 2009.

Describes an episode of the PBS science program Nova featuring a biography of Feynman, currently available in video.

Feynman, Richard. "Cargo Cult Science." Available online. URL: http://calteches.library.caltech.edu/51/2/CargoCult.htm. Accessed May 10, 2009.

Feynman's remarks from his 1974 Caltech commencement address. Feynman gives examples of how scientists can fool themselves and mislead others.

"Feynman Online." Available online. URL: http://www.feynmanonline.com/. Accessed December 5, 2009.

Offers news and resources about Feynman and his work, including groups involved in ongoing activities.

"Friends of Tuva." Available online. URL: http://www.fotuva.org/etc/contact.html. Accessed December 7, 2009.

An organization that grew out of Feynman's long interest in the remote Asian republic of Tannu Tuva. The group was developed by Feynman's friend Ralph Leighton, author of Tuva or Bust!

Halber, Deborah. "Scientists Remember Feynman as New Book Is Published." MIT News Office. Available online. URL: http://web.mit.edu/newsoffice/1998/print/feynman-0520-print.html. Accessed March 19, 2009.

Recollections of Feynman's early years at MIT in connection with the publication of Feynman's book The Meaning of It All: Thoughts of a Citizen-Scientist.

Langston, Peter. "Fun People" [Archive]. "Feynman bowling-ball anecdote & two offspring." Available online. URL: http://www.langston.com/Fun_People/1994/1994ABX.html. Accessed May 22, 2009.

Tells the story of how Feynman's demonstration of conservation laws went dangerously awry when conducted by an experienced teacher.

"The Pleasure of Finding Things Out." *BBC Horizon/PBS Nova,* 1981. Available online. URL: http://video.google.com/videoplay?docid=87773 81378502286852&hl=en. Accessed December 7, 2009.

> *Documentary interview with Richard Feynman in 1981. Feynman describes his love of science and tells many stories about his life.*

"QED: A Play About Richard Feynman." *The Science Show.* Available online. URL: http://www.abc.net.au/rn/scienceshow/ stories/2008/2234039.htm. Accessed December 10, 2009.

> *An interview with Henri Szeps, who plays Richard Feynman in a play based on incidents from the physicist's life.*

"Richard Feynman Playing Bongos." YouTube. Available online. URL: http://www.youtube.com/watch?v=HKTSaezB4p8. Accessed December 7, 2009.

> *Feynman and a friend play the bongos and sing.*

"Richard P. Feynman and the Feynman Diagrams." U.S. Department of Energy. Available online. URL: http://www.osti.gov/accomplishments/ feynman.html. Accessed December 1, 2009.

> *A collection of resources and links relating to Feynman's work. Includes links to Feynman's scientific papers.*

Periodicals

Dyson, Freeman. "Wise Man." *New York Review of Books,* vol. 52, October 20, 2005. Available online. URL: http://www.nybooks.com/ articles/article-preview?article_id=18350. Accessed December 1, 2009.

> *Reviews* Perfectly Reasonable Deviations from the Beaten Track: The Letters of Richard Feynman *and includes the reviewer's personal reminiscences of Feynman.*

Feynman, Richard. "What Is Science?" *The Physics Teacher,* vol. 7, 1968. Available online. URL: http://www.fotuva.org/feynman/what_is_ science.html. Accessed March 1, 2009.

> *Reprint of a talk originally given to the National Science Teachers Association, In it Feynman explains how many textbooks teach definitions rather than helping students really think about nature.*

Feynman, Michelle. "The Feynman File: His Daughter's Archive Offers a Wormhole into the Secret Life of a Charismatic Physicist." *Discover,* vol. 26, March 2005, p. 46 ff.

Includes highlights of many Feynman letters later edited and published by Michelle Feynman in Perfectly Reasonable Deviations from the Beaten Track.

Hillis, W. Daniel. "Richard Feynman and the Connection Machine." *Physics Today,* December 1989. Available online. URL: http://www. longnow.org/views/essays/articles/ArtFeynman.php. Accessed on December 10, 2009.

Describes how computer scientist Daniel Hillis met Richard Feynman through Feynman's son, Carl, who was studying computers. Feynman would play a key role in designing the world's first "massively parallel" computer, the connection machine.

Isherwood, Charles. *QED. Variety,* November 26, 2001, p. 31.

Review of a play by Peter Parnell based on the writings and adventures of Richard Feynman. Set toward the end of Feynman's life, the play features incidents from the book Tuva or Bust! *and the physicist's final exploration of the big questions of life.*

Johnson, George. "Jaguar and the Fox." *Atlantic Monthly,* July 2000, pp. 82–85. Available online. URL: http://www.theatlantic.com/issues/2000/07/johnson.htm. Accessed December 1, 2009.

Contrasts Feynman and Murray Gell-Mann, who lived many years in his shadow, leading to some resentment. Gell-Mann considers Feynman to have been a great physicist, but somewhat overrated.

Kennedy, J. Michael. "The Cult of Richard Feynman: His Peculiar Immortality Springs from More Than His Scientific Achievements." *Los Angeles Times* magazine, Dec. 2, 2001, p. 16.

Describes how Feynman's largely self-made reputation as an eccentric has survived, making him a kind of scientific pop star.

Kruglinski, Susan. "The *Discover* Interview: Murray Gell-Mann." *Discover,* April 2009, pp. 66–73.

An interview with the discoverer of quarks whose office was next door to Feynman's for many years. Gell-Mann assesses Feynman as "pretty good, but not as good as he thought he was."

Weiss, Peter Ulrich. "Dr. Feynman's Doodles: How One Scientist's Simple Sketches Transformed Physics." *Science News,* July 16, 2005, p. 40 ff.

Describes the profoundly useful Feynman diagrams and how they helped a generation of physicists understand quantum electrodynamics.

Welton, Theodore A. "Memories of Feynman." *Physics Today*, February 2007, pp. 46–52.

> *The author, a close friend and colleague of Feynman, recalls incidents from college, Los Alamos, and later.*

INDEX